Contest Judo

Contest Judo

ROY INMAN, 6th Dan

with Nicolas Soames

The Crowood Press

First published in 1987 by
The Crowood Press
Ramsbury, Marlborough
Wiltshire SN8 2HE

British Library Cataloguing in Publication Data

Inman, Roy
   Contest judo.
   1. Judo
   I. Title   II. Soames, Nicolas
   796.8'152   GV1114

ISBN 1 85223 076 2

Picture Credits

Line illustrations by Lesley Sayer
Photographs by David Finch

Typeset by Qualitext Typesetting Abingdon
Printed in Great Britain at the University Printing House, Oxford

Contents

Foreword

While the techniques of judo are displayed in a thousand different ways, the essence remains the same. In that sense, the central ideas enshrined in the Gokyo are as valid today as they ever were. But modern sports conditions make different demands, and if judo is not to ossify it must adapt – and adaptation in the face of change is one of the most fundamental features of judo itself.

Throughout the past century, judo has demonstrated its ability to keep pace with these demands. This book sets out to look at the main throwing techniques that are used at the highest competitive levels today. Some of them are truly innovative – ingenious solutions to the problems set by the prevailing contest conditions created by men and women who are stronger, fitter and more gymnastically aware than ever before. Other techniques appear new to this generation, but are really old, half-forgotten ideas resurfacing and proving as effective as they were decades ago.

Contest Judo is presented by Roy Inman, for over ten years the manager of the highly successful women's team. A former British international, he has kept closely in touch with the development of both men's and women's judo. His alert judo observation makes this imaginative book invaluable to the modern judoka.

Syd Hoare
Chairman, British Judo Association

Acknowledgements

Judo photography is notoriously difficult. The photographer can be in the right place at the right time but, without an intimate understanding of contest judo, can fail to catch the right moment.

David Finch is without doubt one of the most distinguished judo specialists active today. Since 1972 he has photographed every European Championships except the 1976 event, and every Olympic and World Championships except 1983. That alone is a remarkable record.

The results can be seen on virtually every page of this book. It is no exaggeration to say that this book would have been impossible without the generous access to his remarkable portfolio. He has seen the emergence of many outstanding champions. As a 1st Dan member of The Budokwai, London, he himself practised regularly with such figures as Angelo Parisi and later Neil Adams, and regards them, along with others such as Jean Paul Coche, Bernard Tchoullyan and Karen Briggs, as among the most photogenic of fighters.

If he is forced to single out one photograph from nearly two decades of work, he opts for that remarkable *Harai-goshi* executed by Guy Auffray which can be seen on page 105. Everything is right: the light, the focus, but above all the inimitable feeling that the essence of judo – which seems so ephemeral – is caught in that one frame.

Other thanks go to John Hennessy and Peter Inman who were willing ukes for the video work which led to Lesley Sayer's patient artistic work; Charles Palmer, Chairman of the British Olympic Association and President of the British Judo Association for help with the history chapter; and the BJA itself (with Tony Reay in particular), Richard Bowen and Syd Hoare for archival material.

Introduction

Contest represents the cutting edge of that huge conglomeration of history and hopes, of aspirations, of techniques, and of theory that makes up the rich and varied world of judo. And there is little question that what happens on the competition mat of the Olympic Games or the World Championships gradually, though it may take some time, filters down through the national organisations to the local clubs.

The years have shown that judo is one of the liveliest sports in terms of innovation, and one of the richest in terms of sheer variety of techniques. In fact, judo is moving so quickly that it is almost as difficult for a coach to keep up to date with the latest ideas as the computer expert struggling with new marvels every week.

Since its foundation in 1882 judo has never stood still, because the demands of contest have dictated change. Predictability means defeat in judo which is why new techniques are emerging to join battle with older techniques once forgotten but now newly resurrected. Of course, the basic principles remain largely the same, and therefore there will always be a need for books covering the judo alphabet. But there has also been a real need for a book to document, however briefly and incompletely, the judo techniques that are being used now in top competitions. Some are very similar to those throws we learned as beginners; some are the same – change for change's sake has little place in judo; others are so weird and complex that they look impractical in the extreme. But all the techniques introduced in this book have one factor in common – they can be seen working successfully in many of the top competitions for men and women throughout the world.

The danger of this book is that it starts to go out of date as soon as it is published – and there is no doubt that judo is developing quickly. In every major championship I attend I expect to see something that surprises me. As a result, I have not been able to include everything that is being used – that would be an unwieldy list – and have chosen to concentrate on tachiwaza (the throws) rather than attempt to include newaza (the groundwork) as well. To cover both would be too large a task for a book of this kind. However, I have included two techniques to show how closely linked are tachiwaza and newaza.

Most of all, I hope that this book reflects my admiration for the remarkable manner in which judo refuses to be ossified, but rather, through its very nature, forces its participants to think and re-evaluate in a constantly creative manner. This is why judo has been, for me, such a totally absorbing study for twenty-five years.

Roy Inman

3

1 The Changing Face of Judo

It has been said that judo is one of the very few sports where, after twenty years of active involvement, it is possible to go to a competition and still see something totally new. Sometimes it is just a minor adjustment to a grip or an entry which is nevertheless sufficient to bring to life a technique previously written off as old-fashioned and easily stopped. Sometimes, it is the combination of something old with something new. Or it could be a question of the cycle of fashion, with people forgetting defences and counters to some old throws that were toppling our judo grandfathers. More rarely, it is a real innovation, which sets in train a series of new ideas based on the same theme.

What is clear is that these new or refreshed ideas usually come not so much from casual randori or the normal teaching situation, but from the hothouse of the contest judo environment. It is in the heat of contest that the viability of judo techniques in the modern context is really tested. And judo is, above all, intensely pragmatic. If the opponent does not go over, and the fitness and timing of the thrower is not at fault, adjustments need to be made to the technique itself. It is as simple as that.

If, of course, the basic ways of doing the throws in the Gokyo worked on the Olympic mat, there would be no need for change. But the fact is that, over the years, opponents learned to stop many of the fundamental techniques and, necessity being the mother of invention, canny players came up with variations that allowed them to break through

defences and produce ippon. There were those who felt strongly committed to maintaining what they felt was the true tradition of judo, who continued to take hold of their opponent with both hands and do judo in what they felt was a gentlemanly, upright manner. That was fine, so long as they were prepared to take their medicine if they could not make their traditional judo work and breakfall. In the old samurai days, the answer was much simpler. Those die-hards who stuck to their old-fashioned techniques died.

Many of the traditionalists seemed to forget that Kano himself was a great innovator, and that the strong contest men of those first two decades of judo such as Saigo and Yamashita were creating new techniques nearly every time they stepped on the mat. In fact, Kano felt that adaptability rather than dogmatism was one of the hallmarks of a judo man.

This principle was seen in action when the fighters from the Soviet Union first entered contest judo in the late 1950s. They were accustomed to their own wrestling style, sambo, where the emphasis was placed on throwing with belt grips and all kinds of leg grabs and pick-ups, and where armlocks were the most common form of achieving a submission. Judo competitors brought up in the Japanese tradition, who were accustomed to maintain what was felt to be a good posture and who were as concerned to see the grade of the opponent as well as the size, were suddenly being put square on their backs with an unorthodox leg grab by a man with a white belt. Though it was not viewed very favourably at the time, this gave judo a profound jolt, and it says much about the sport itself that it was able to weather the storm and questions about the very nature of judo and emerge, stronger than ever, in the last decades of the twentieth century.

It is also worth noting that the Russians discovered, as time passed, that the basic judo principles were in fact as good, if not better, than many of the sambo tricks. Ever ready to incorporate the best ideas wherever they found them, it became evident from the *Uchimatas* and *Tai-otoshis* that appeared on the international contest mat, done by Russian players, that traditional judo ideas were taking root in the Soviet Union. It could be argued that, ironically, some of the best examples of traditional judo seen on the contest mat in the 1980s have come from fighters from the Soviet Union. On the other hand, judo in the Oriental East and particularly the European West has benefitted from the special study of armlocks made in Moscow.

Contest judo dictated the need for continuous change but not necessarily for innovation. Trends and fashion in judo are as significant as innovation. Some years ago *Seoi-nage* in its standing form was a high-scoring contest technique. Then the defences against it became so strong that, in more recent years, *Drop Seoi-nage* has dominated. There is little doubt, however, that soon fighters will become so accustomed to the feeling of the drop that it will prove much less effective, and the time will be ripe for one person to come along with a slightly different way of making standing *Seoi-nage* work again. This cyclical trend is seen again and again in judo.

Of course, it is possible to win one or even two competitions on a couple of tricks. But only those tricks which have a real grounding in fundamental judo principles, and which therefore could be called techniques in their own right, will survive one or two outings.

However, judo techniques have been affected not only by learned defences but by other aspects of the hothouse environment of contest, especially as judo contest changed to take into account modern values and attitudes, both to life and to sport.

FITNESS

In the decade from 1970 to 1980 there was a truly dramatic increase in the level of fitness of fighters on the international contest mat, and relative increases in the fitness of competitors at national and even area level. Even in the 1960s it was common to see light-heavyweights with substantial protruding stomachs. In short, they were carrying fat. There were a few who were in good physical shape but on the whole they were not. By 1980 every major light-heavyweight was a fit athlete who could boast washboard abdominals. The heavyweights, who need bulk, are a different case, although nowadays even many heavyweights have a high level of fitness.

This has partly been the result of a much better understanding of the whole meaning of fitness in the judo world. The traditional view was that the best way to get fit for judo was to do judo. This was simply not true because of the high rate of injuries in judo when a player is training at top level. It proved impossible to do the amount of judo needed to achieve the required physical standard without getting the knocks and muscle strains that would set the training programme back a few weeks.

Supplementary training, particularly running and weight training, with schedules culled from other sports ranging from boxing and athletics to swimming and gymnastics, drastically raised the fitness of judo competitors. It took time, but now contest judo players are among the fittest sportsmen and women in the world.

Such improved fitness also raised the standard of the judo itself. Weight training produced greater explosive power and cut down on injuries, while improved aerobic rates meant that fighters could attack harder for longer periods. Other modern aspects of training, such as intelligent use of crashmat work, meant that greater technical as well as physical demands could be made upon the players.

All this led to the obvious fact that better use could be made of the randori time, with specific technical tasks being set, rather than coping with randori as a fitness medium as well as a learning situation.

WEIGHT CATEGORIES

The introduction of weight categories over the decades has also made a strong impact on judo on many levels. Primarily, it has made judo more not less skilful. At the start of the contest, two fighters face each other on an equal basis. They know that they weigh the same, they are – or should be – equally fit and presumably equally strong, and the only thing that separates them is their skill and tactical awareness. Therefore, the onus is on the improvement of the skill factors.

Just how much this has improved judo skills at all weights can be seen from the fact that it is rare, now, to see an 80 kilo player make any real headway against a light-heavyweight or heavyweight in an open competition. The light-heavyweights and heavyweights have improved so much that it is not often that the disparity in skill is sufficient to make up for the difference in weight. Even as relatively recently as the 1960s and the early 1970s, this was not necessarily the case.

So now, when competitors face each other with equal weight, strength, experience and skill, sometimes it is only a mental strength, a will to win, unpredictability, or, most common of all, tactical awareness, that separates the victor from the loser.

RULES

Contest rules have existed in judo almost since its foundation. They were initially introduced largely as a safety measure, to prevent the many serious injuries that were occurring. An additional factor was to promote the throwing aspects of judo as well as the newaza. (Ju-jitsu schools specialising in groundwork were entering those early contests with the Kano's Kodokan Judo school with the sole aim of dragging the opponent to the ground in any way and polishing him off with a strangle, lock or hold.)

Injuries to the knees in contests resulted in the ban of leg locks. Similarly, injuries to internal organs resulted in the ban of *Dojime*, or the kidney squeeze. These were drastic examples of the way changes in contest rules affected the techniques of judo itself, showing how the experience of contest paved the way for judo in the wider sense.

However, even small changes to contest rules affected normal judo randori. The introduction of the rule forbidding a contestant to hold his opponent's belt for long periods was introduced in an attempt to prevent negative defence, but it changed the way throws such as *Tsuri-goshi* were approached. The rule disallowing the holding of the sleeve and lapel on the same side for any longer than a few seconds – introduced again for reasons of negative defence – also affected the practice of a whole range of throws, including *Yama-arashi*, which now have to be attempted as soon as the grip is taken.

The shortening of the duration of fights – regretted by many traditionalists who preferred 15 or 20 minute finals (the finals of the All-Japan Championships are still 10 minutes) – and the introduction of passivity rules meant, paradoxically, that a greater not lesser level of fitness was required. Passivity rules increased the pace of the fights which, though shorter, did not allow the long periods of inactivity tolerated in a longer contest.

Other rules, including the banning of

fingers inside the jacket or trousers, and the lengthening of jacket sleeves to a required size, all had their effects on techniques: bringing some into favour and putting others out to grass — until a fresh idea or change of rules resulted in a rethink. Even the stepping out rule made judo players more tactically aware, and prevented players snatching a breather by 'arranging' to go off the fighting area. Inevitably, all these changes affected the way judo was practised in the clubs throughout the world.

Many traditionalists feel strongly that the introduction of koka and yuko has been detrimental to judo, but I do not agree. In the hundreds of international matches I have attended, I have never seen a player go out with the express intention of winning on a koka. Fighters were just as reluctant to be knocked down in the pre-koka days because they knew that, in the event of a draw, it would count in the referee's mind.

In fact, the small scores can add to dramatic judo, for if a player scores a koka a minute from the end of a contest, his opponent must open up in an attempt to level the score, thus increasing the chances for a really decisive technique.

DIFFERENT STYLES

The development of international competition has also brought a new appraisal of style to judo. Traditionally, it was regarded as good style to stand up straight, take a grip with both hands, and fight like a gentleman. Someone who bent over double, walked around like a gorilla with one hand swinging free, waiting for the counter opportunity, was regarded derogatorily as a lurker. The man who grabbed at anything and everything, prepared to fight tooth and nail for any little knockdown or fall over, was derided as a mauler. Gradually, though, it became apparent that often this was simply another style of judo, just as worthy of respect as the traditional style, and frequently extremely effective. After all, judo reflects different personalities in similar ways to other human activities.

Even the judo fighters who prided themselves on being technicians had to learn to adapt to bent postures, sideways postures, double lapel grips, throws off one grip — and they did, of course, often innovating at the same time. Thus judo became an even richer repository of technique as a result. It could also be argued that most of these styles have been tried in judo in its earlier history and, as always, the styles that survive are those that work. In the end, it comes down to Kano's old maxim of maximum effect with minimum effort.

THE LEARNING CURVE

The most important single lesson modern contest judo at international level has taught is that it is impossible to go out into contest hoping to find an idiot at the end of your arms. Contests, especially failure in contests, teach people to think (although most people can produce exceptions to the rule!) and most international players are not fighting robots who can be put back in the cupboard after the event or occasionally put back into the workshop for repairs. They are thinking fighters and this leads directly to change and development, as the developments of *Tomoe-nage* have shown.

In the 1960s and 1970s *Tomoe-nage* was never a really high scorer in international competition, although it always had its adherents. The difficulty was that the classic over-the-top technique meant that uke spent a considerable amount of time in the air, and the improving fitness, strength and gymnastic training resulted in many top players learning to spin out.

Gradually, other forms of *Tomoe-nage* appeared in contest — the varying kinds of *Yoko-tomoe-nage* that cut down the amount of time uke spent in the air, making the direction of the throw much more unpredictable. Now, even the old form of *Tomoe-nage* has its success rate, because players are getting so accustomed to expecting a *Yoko-tomoe* that, to their immense frustration, they are finding they are being caught on a classic.

A similar tale can be told for *Kata-guruma*, with the direction of throw now being more frequently to the rear than over the side. This development, incidentally, has also been made more possible by the intelligent use of crashmats.

There are those who follow fashion and those who create it. This is where contest judo is truly creative. For example, the striking popularity of *Uchimata* in its various forms over the past twenty years or so suggests that the wheel is about to turn. Are fighters becoming so accustomed to 'riding' or predicting an *Uchimata* that junior players poised to enter the international scene would be better employed concentrating on a throw that makes use of an *Uchimata* defence? For instance, as fighters are now effective in defending against *Uchimata* attacks on the near thigh, or straight up the middle, is it now time to work on a slightly changed *Hane-goshi* – for years discarded as ineffective in modern judo – which would attack the far leg?

With contest judo constantly pushing into new horizons, the learning curve in judo never stops. Once it does, it ossifies, and players lose. It is as simple as that.

INJURIES

The involvement of judo in the international sports arena through competition has resulted in a much better understanding of injuries. The traditional attitude, of continuing to train with quite serious injuries in some misguided belief in the character-building aspects of no pain, no gain, has been supplanted by a better awareness of what should be rested and what can be safely bandaged and ignored.

JUDO AS SPORT

In one sense, contest judo has seen a major change in the whole attitude towards judo as an activity, which in part reflects a change in the values of society. From Kano's point of view contest was just one aspect of judo, on a level of equal importance with kata and randori. For Kano judo was a means for the education of the personality, and concentration on competition for the sake of medals, public kudos or money was seriously frowned upon.

There is no doubt that attitudes towards contest in this sense have changed. Very few contestants entering the Olympics will have a regular formal kata practice (*Nage-no-kata*, *Katame-no-kata* and so on) although surprisingly few would feel that kata is such a complete waste of time that it should be abolished. The difference is, perhaps, one of defined purpose.

International contest is so demanding that it requires full-time commitment to have any real chance of success. The defined goal of the sportsman is to push ahead the frontiers of one area of judo. He is prepared to work hard in the sport – and no one who has maintained an international-level training programme can say that it is without its hardships and its pain. But he is not prepared to endure quantity – such as a three-hour randori practice – where he will be forced to sacrifice quality. He needs to learn to work at peak, not to cruise without being thrown.

However, this does not prevent others, with other attitudes and other goals, to make of judo a wider study. The meeting place is the randori where a real exchange can take place. It is interesting to note that a glance at judo history suggests that, even in its early days, there seemed to be a distinct difference between those judoka fighting at the top level and those more concerned with the educational aspects of judo. One wonders whether very much has changed.

There is no doubt that contest is the research department of judo. Take it away, and it will lose its future. It has already shown itself remarkably able to accommodate change and, in fact, has emerged stronger than ever. What follows are just a few of the results of those changes.

2 Contest Techniques

TE-GURUMA

Te-guruma (direct attack)
(Hand wheel)

Introduction

Te-guruma is normally considered a counter-technique, but has proved to be equally effective as a direct attack.

Weight categories

All weights.

Opportunity

Static, eyeball to eyeball situation. Upright posture.

Grips

Middle lapel and rear outside thigh.

Entry

As hand grips thigh, leading leg makes a half-circle to place tori sideways on to uke.

Lift

Tori lifts uke and pulls in tight to achieve good body contact.

Direction

Once uke is airborne, the lapel grip pulls down and circles.

Tips

1. It is important to get the head free of uke's controlling arm. When tori ducks his head under, he must push uke's arm up at the same time.
2. Get maximum height on the lift. Because of the lapel grip, uke will attempt to prevent the throw by getting a hand down, so height of lift is an important factor.

Andreas Paluschek (East Germany) gets a good lift from Te-guruma *used as a direct attack at the 1986 European Championships in Belgrade.*

Te-guruma (counter)

Introduction

Contrary to general opinion, this need not necessarily be a spontaneous counter. It can be practised in order to counter the attack of a particular opponent.

Weight categories

All weights.

Grips

High lapel.

Opportunity

It is used mainly against throws on one leg such as *Uchimata* or *Harai-goshi*, but it will work effectively against other throws, like *Ippon-seoi-nage*.

When Te-guruma *is used as a counter, if the lift is not high, the rotation becomes crucial, as demonstrated in competition by Roy Inman against the Korean H. Cho.*

Entry

Tori must be able to maintain a stable stance despite uke's attack, otherwise the danger is that he will get caught by the original attack, even if he manages to get the lifting hand in position.

Lift

The lifting hand establishes a strong body contact before the lifting action begins. Once uke has been lifted high – and the higher the better – virtually all the rotation comes from the lapel grip.

Tip

The better the lift, the less uke will be able to frustrate the throw by hooking on to tori.

13

OSOTO–GAKE/GARI

Osoto-gake
(Major outer hook)

(a)

(b)

Weight categories

All weights.

Introduction

It is important to be absolutely clear of the fundamental difference between *Osoto-gake* and *Osoto-gari*. Of course, *gake* means hook and *gari* means reap, but this is not enough. It must be appreciated that in a *gake* throw the working leg is the back leg, the attacking leg only hooks on. In a *gari* throw the working leg is the attacking or reaping leg.

Grips

Many different grips can be used, from normal sleeve and high collar to sleeve and lapel, or middle lapel and high lapel.

Entry

The attacking leg hooks, the arms pull uke's body round on to tori, and then the back leg can begin to drive.

Tip

Tori should be looking clearly at the point of the mat where he intends to deposit his opponent. This is important for many throws, but especially here, in order to focus the direction of throwing effort. Continuing the *gake* action tori drives straight down, but often the initial *gake* action can then turn into a *gari* action so the hooking leg then sweeps.

Three different examples of Osoto-gake, *each clearly showing a stage in the action. (a) The opening hook. (b) The follow-through and strong drive which enables Angelo Parisi to throw the Soviet Olympic Champion Shoto Chochosvilli. (c) And the finish – with Parisi this time on the receiving end.*

(c)

Osoto-gari
(Major outer reap)

Weight categories

Middleweights and above.

Opportunity

Against a reasonably upright opponent with the leg to be attacked slightly advanced.

Entry

Classical entry, with tori's hips pushing past uke followed by a driving see-saw action with head down and leg up.

Timing

Tori initiates the attacking movement by pulling uke on to the advanced foot. As uke resists, tori steps forward and sweeps with the other leg.

Direction of throw

This is *not* directly to the rear, at least not at the beginning of the throw. Instead, tori directs the throw off at an angle of about 45 degrees. The mechanics of the movement may, once uke is airborne, direct the throw directly to uke's rear.

Tips

Osoto-gari generally fails because uke's head has not been controlled. If a lapel grip is taken, uke's jaw-bone must be controlled by tori's lapel-grip hand. If a high collar is preferred, the inside of the arm must control the head. Failure to do this not only makes the attack ineffective, but leaves tori open to a counter.

Brian Jacks with a textbook Osoto-gari *finish, producing an incontrovertible ippon at the British Open 1977.*

Osoto-gari (arm over)

Weight categories

All weights.

Grips

Sleeve grip.

Entry

Like so many *Osotos*, the initial attack is a *gake*, a hook. Tori takes hold of the sleeve and, before uke can stabilise, attacks, hooking on to uke's leg. As he hooks, he brings his other arm over uke's arm and clamps as if to prepare for a *Makikomi*-type throw, but the whole direction of the attack continues towards uke's back corner.

Throwing action

With uke's weight firmly committed to one foot, tori can hop further round uke and change the attacking action from a *gake* to a *gari*, throwing with a strong reaping movement.

Osoto-gari *with a one-arm grip.*

Ippon-seoi-nage into Osoto-gari
(One-arm shoulder throw into major outer reap)

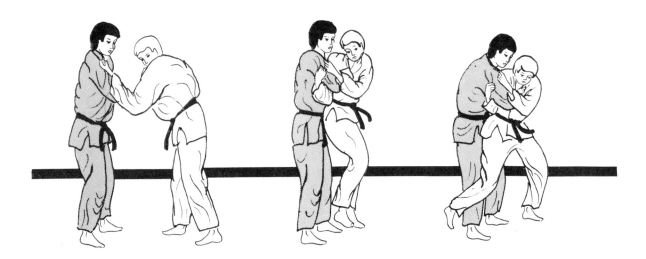

Introduction

This is a combination, but one for which tori must aim specifically. It rarely works as a spontaneous reaction, although often it looks as if it is a simple follow-through from a truly committed first attack. In short, tori must set a trap.

Weight categories

Middleweights and below.

Grip

Lapel grip on the side to be attacked, preferably over uke's arm.

Entry

Tori feints a normal *Ippon-seoi* attack to the front, but does not take his hip too far through and does not place his right foot (in a right-handed throw) on the ground. His right leg must be a kind of floating leg which, once uke blocks, can immediately curl and hook on to uke's leg. Tori then hops round, using his chin on uke's trapped arm for extra control.

Direction of throw

Awareness of the placing of the chin also aids the throwing action, for it makes tori aware of exactly where he is to throw his opponent – to the rear corner or directly back, according to where his eyes are pointing.

Ippon-seoi-nage *mixed with* Osoto-gake.

Osoto-otoshi to Nidan-kosoto-gari
(Major outer drop to two-step minor outer reap)

Weight categories

Middleweights and above.

Grips

High lapel, low sleeve.

Entry

The movement starts with a conventional *Osoto-gari* that fails because of the lack of head control. Uke starts to counter with *Osoto-gaeshi*. At this point tori places his right foot (in a right-handed technique) on the ground, turns to his right, and sweeps uke's left leg at the back of the knee.

Kouchi-gari countered by Osoto-gari
(Minor inner reap countered by major outer reap)

Weight categories

Middleweights and below.

Grips

Double lapel, but with the over-arm grip on the same side as the eventual *Osoto-gari* attack.

Entry

Tori sets the trap by leaving his foot slightly forward, inviting a *Kouchi*. As uke attacks, he takes the foot away by bending at the knee – not withdrawing the whole leg which is a large movement – and attacking immediately with *Osoto-gari*.

Throwing action

It is the momentum of uke's attack, missing tori's leg, which actually starts the throwing action.

OUCHI-GARI/GAKE

Ouchi-gake
(Major inner hook)

Weight categories

All weights.

Opportunity

Opponent is bent over in *Jigotai* position.

Grips

Low sleeve, middle lapel.

Attack

The attacking leg hooks strongly behind uke's knee or even above.

Direction of throw

This can vary. Uke can either be thrown directly back, with the main force coming strongly from the back leg. Or, as the photograph shows, the opponent can be taken over the other leg, driving his whole weight over the side of the foot.

Tip

In this second case, the head needs to be controlled. For the conventional rear direction, tori's elbow pushes forcefully against uke's chest.

Japan's Michinori Ishibasi drives his Ouchi-gake *over the standing leg for a major score in the 1975 World Championships. Note head control.*

Ouchi-gake (lunge)

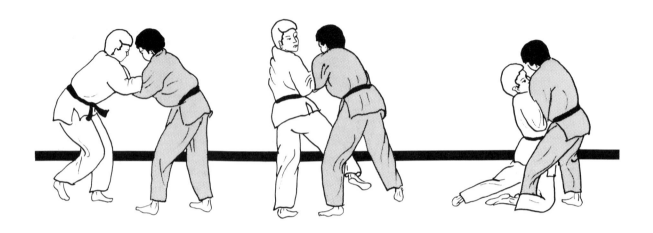

Weight categories

All weights.

Grips

Tori should take sleeve and middle lapel, but with the lapel-grip arm outside uke's arm. Tori's arm pushes against uke's wrist, thus trapping the arm. This gives tori more control during the throw and enables him to prevent uke twisting out of the throw.

Entry

This can be compared to the classic fencer's lunge. The hooking leg takes uke's leg well below the knee and, at the same time, tori's bodyweight sinks low. It is this dropping action that pins uke's foot to the mat.

Sakaguchi (Japan) demonstrates the principle of the lunging Ouchi-gake.

Ouchi-gari (hand assisted)
(Major inner reap)

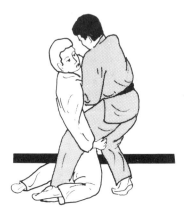

Weight categories

Middleweights and below.

Grips

Lapel, sleeve. It must be possible to release the lapel grip quickly.

Entry

This begins as a standard *Ouchi-gari* attack. Often, uke is able to step off the reaping foot, which is why this throw was developed. Immediately, tori releases the lapel grip and drops the hand to pick up uke's leg just behind the knee. He must control the leg before uke can stabilise on it.

Throwing action

It is this sudden blocking action of the hand which takes uke over backwards.

World Champion Karen Briggs (Britain) has just caught the heel of Loly Verguillas (Spain), in the stretched Ouchi-gake *lunge, but it is the hand that finally destroys her opponent's balance and brings the score.*

Ouchi-gari with leg pick-up

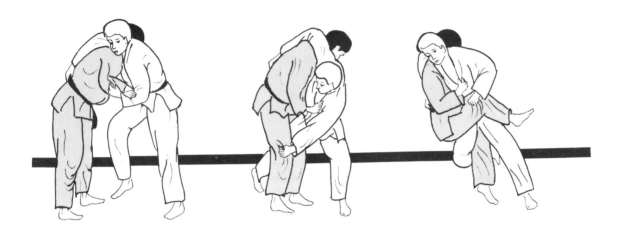

Weight categories

All weights.

Grips

One arm over the shoulder holding belt, sleeve.

Entry

Uke must feel a forward throw is coming. Tori attacks with *Ouchi-gari* and, as uke attempts to stabilise on the other leg, tori releases his sleeve grip and grasps the trouser leg.

Throwing action

This is aided forcefully by the lift from the trouser grip.

Tip

This can be combined with a *Tsuri-goshi* or the *Uranage* combination with hip throw.

It takes the added refinement of the leg grab for Britain's Ray Stevens to finally take his opponent backwards.

Ogoshi to Ouchi-gari
(Major hip throw to major inner reap)

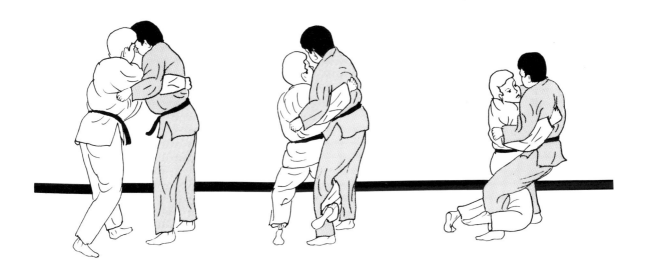

Weight categories

All weights.

Grips

Round the waist, sleeve or lapel.

Entry

The grips suggest an *Ogoshi* attempt, but tori turns in directly for the *Ouchi-gari*.

Throwing action

The lunge action helps to sink uke's weight on his attacked foot; tori's arm around the waist controls uke's hips, and nullifies any attempt to twist out.

ASHI-DORI

Morote-gari
(Double hand reap)

Weight categories

All weights.

Opportunity

Surprise technique to be used against a relatively upright opponent. Tori approaches as if to take a standard grip.

Grips

Both arms grip above the knees.

Entry

While feinting for the normal grip, tori suddenly steps in with a lunging action on one leg and grabs both uke's legs. The action should be pull and lift.

Direction of throw

Uke can be thrown directly to the rear, but more often than not the direction is slightly to one side or the other.

Tip

To inject more impetus into the throw, bring the shoulder into uke's abdomen.

. . . whereas here uke has managed to twist well before the grip was taken.

The Morote-gari *has been taken high up on the opponent's thighs, so that although the balance and direction is not ideal, a complete defensive turn-out is unlikely . . .*

Ashi-dori
(Leg grab)

Weight categories

All weights.

Grip

One hand holds middle lapel.

Opportunity

This works best when both players are in bent posture, with opposing stances, left against right.

Entry

Grab behind the knee on the same side as the lapel grip. At the same time, step in for a *Tani-otoshi* position.

*Jean-Michel Berthet (France) scores with an unorthodox leg grab in the
final of the British Open 1986.*

Ashi-dori
(Back leg grab)

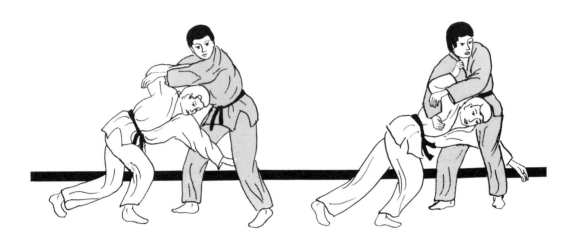

Weight categories

All weights.

Grips

Cross grip, on the opposite side of the leg to
be attacked.

Opportunity

Tori must be in a bent posture, facing an
opponent who has one foot quite markedly in
front of the other.

Entry

Uke will be stabilised strongly on the back leg
and not expecting an attack from so far away.
Tori scoops under the arms to pick up the
back leg behind the knee and then drives
forward.

Throwing action

This sudden destabilisation can tip uke quite
easily on to his back.

Ashi-dori
(Over-arm inside leg grab)

Weight categories

All weights.

Grip

One sleeve.

Entry

Tori enters as if for *Makikomi*. But instead of winding in, he takes his armpit over uke's arm and brings it backwards to hook inside the leg.

Throwing action

At this point, tori simply sits down, throwing his legs out. The feel of the throw is a *Kouchi-gake* with the hand. It is a frustrating one to be caught with, for though a complex movement, once tori is in position there is no escape.

Comment

This normally does not produce a big score, just a koka or yuko. But there are times when a small koka can be as crucial as an ippon.

Tani-otoshi (arm over)
(Valley drop)

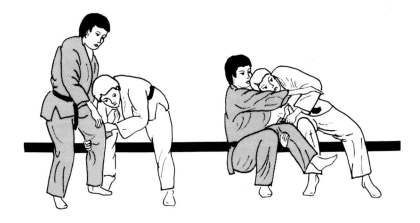

Dawn Netherwood (Great Britain) wins her 1984 World Bronze Medal with a minor score from this unusual Tani-otoshi.

Weight categories

Middleweights and below.

Grips

Over-arm lapel grip, other hand takes low sleeve on the same side.

Entry

Tori pulls strongly on sleeve grip to bring uke's weight on to advanced foot. Immediately, tori releases sleeve grip and brings the elbow over and, stepping in towards uke, picks up near leg behind the knee. It is important that at this stage tori should have his back against uke, with the back of his head firmly placed against uke's chest. This prevents uke bending forward to escape the throw.

Throwing action

Tori pulls on the leg and, pushing with the back of his head, executes a sacrifice throw.

Tip

The simple avoidance to the throw is for uke to take the threatened leg back. If it is evident to tori that uke is aware of this avoidance, he can precede the *Tani-otoshi* attack with a *Kouchi-gari* feint.

Kouchi-gari-ashi-dori
(Minor inner reap leg grab)

Opportunity

Tori should be in a slightly bent posture.

Entry

Tori steps wide with left foot (in a right-handed throw) and makes a *Kouchi-gari* attack, which uke steps off. But before uke can settle, tori's empty hand picks up uke's leg, preferably at knee or rear-thigh level. This breaks uke's balance.

Weight categories

All weights.

Grips

Cross lapel, leaving one arm free.

Throwing action

The force of the throw comes from the cross-grip arm driving over towards the rear corner, where he would naturally use his other leg to brace were tori not controlling it with his hand.

The hand-assisted Kouchi-gari *is used by both men and women, as shown here by World Light-middleweight Champion Neil Adams (Great Britain) . . .*

. . . and World Bantamweight Silver Medallist Marie-France Colignon (France).

Uchimata-ashi-dori
(Inner thigh into leg grab sacrifice throw)

Introduction

This is a rather complicated combination, so the drawings show a left attack, while the photograph shows a right attack, to aid fighters of both stances.

Weight categories

All weights.

Grips

Back of jacket, low sleeve.

Entry

Tori attempts an *Uchimata* against an upright posture, but makes sure that the supporting leg is outside uke's stance. Uke blocks. Tori hooks with the lifting *Uchimata* leg in a *Kouchi-gari* action, then lets go of the sleeve grip. He bends down to grab behind uke's leg and lifts.

Throwing action

This puts all uke's weight on his other foot, and a sharp sweeping action with the '*Kouchi*' foot, combined with a sacrifice fall, brings uke sharply and unexpectedly backwards.

Tip

Although this looks like a spontaneous follow-through combination, it can be trained for, because the initial block by an upright uke is extremely common.

Yugoslavia's Obadov (opposite) attacks Coche (France).

KATA-GURUMA

Kata-guruma (cross grip)
(Shoulder wheel)

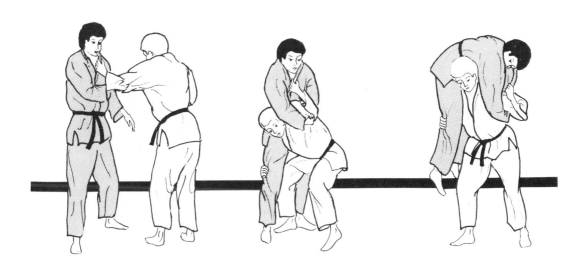

Weight categories

Middleweights and below.

Opportunity

Similar to the straightforward *Kata-guruma*, but the cross grip offers an unexpected entry.

Grips

If tori is attacking the right leg, his left hand holds uke's left lapel.

It looks like a classic Kata-guruma — *but look at the right-hand collar grip.*

Direction of throw

Surprise and confusion of grips can allow a traditional direction of throw, although this does mean that the opponent is in the air for a considerable time and top level players will often spin out.

Kata-guruma (to the rear)

Weight categories

Middleweights and below.

Opportunity

This throw emerges from a fairly static situation with a relatively upright uke, although the grips should be fairly loose, with tori having one hand free.

Grips

Lapel or sleeve and inner thigh.

Direction of throw

The gymnastic abilities of top contestants have made the *Nage-no-kata* form of *Kata-guruma* very rare; even if they are lifted well, opponents find it easy to hook on to prevent the throw, or spin out of the throw in mid-air. Like the classic form of *Tomoe-nage*, uke is simply in the air for too long. The contemporary answer is to unload uke either forwards or, as seen so spectacularly in these photos, backwards.

Training

This should be practised on a crashmat!

Tip

A straight back during the lift is essential.

New directions for Kata-guruma *from (a) Brown (Great Britain) and (b) Vidmayer (Yugoslavia).*

46

(a)

(b)

TAI-OTOSHI

Tai-otoshi (cross grip)
(Body drop)

Weight categories

Middleweights and below.

Opportunity

To be used against a moving not a static opponent.

Grips

Take cross grip – in a right-handed throw, tori's right hand takes the right middle lapel of uke – then take low sleeve. Sleeve can be taken first and middle lapel second.

Entry

Step across opponent with blocking leg, rather than taking a half-circle step backwards and then bringing blocking leg across. What confuses opponent is the double amount of weight on the one arm and shoulder of uke being attacked.

Throwing action

Pull the sleeve in a half-circle to put uke squarely on his back.

Neil Adams (Great Britain) produces a strong whip-action from the cross grip.

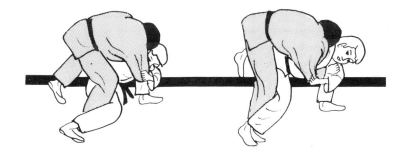

Tai-otoshi (wrong leg)

Weight categories

All weights.

Grips

Double lapel or lapel and sleeve.

Principle

The basic *Tai-otoshi* principles apply here. The only difference is that uke's defence is too strong to allow tori to come right across his opponent for the classic form of the throw, so the attack is made against the near leg, instead of the far leg.

Opportunity

A sideways stance by uke, which would normally prevent a *Tai-otoshi* attack, can signal a good opportunity for this wrong leg version, not least because uke will not expect it.

Entry

The ordinary *Tai-otoshi* entry is made, except that tori's blocking leg aims to block uke's near leg unusually high, preferably on or over the knee. This prevents uke stepping over it easily. Once in, tori rotates as normal.

Throwing action

When the entry has been successfully achieved, the gap between tori and uke allows for a strong rotation, which injects the throwing power into the hands, making it very much a hand throw.

Tip

The turning of the head allows greater rotation.

The 'wrong leg' Tai-otoshi *allowed just enough entry for Britain's Olympic Silver Medallist David Starbrook to use his upper-body strength to power his way through to the conclusion.*

Tai-otoshi (double lapel)

Weight categories

All weights.

Grips

Double lapel.

Opportunity

Uke must be standing slightly at an angle, with, in a left-hand throw, the left leg slightly behind the right.

Entry

Tori steps across to attack uke's back leg. The hands work in the conventional *Tai-otoshi* manner, but the hips and body position are closer to a *Seoi-otoshi*.

Throwing action

Tori's hips block the lower half of uke's body, while tori's hands, working strongly off the lapel grips (which give good control of uke's shoulders and head), bring uke around.

Olympic and World Heavyweight Champion Yasuhiro Yamashita using a double lapel grip to throw with Tai-otoshi.

Tip

Tori's head must turn well to provide room
for a strong rotation.

Uchimata countered by sidestep to Tai-otoshi

(Inner thigh countered by sidestep to body drop)

Weight categories

Middleweights and below.

Grips

Middle lapel, sleeve.

Opportunity

It is rare for this to happen spontaneously. Generally, tori must be aware that his opponent has a strong *Uchimata* and is therefore susceptible to this sidestep counter.

Entry

As uke powers in with a strong *Uchimata*, tori swings his leg forward and to the side (he must not attempt to lift it over) and then immediately attacks with *Tai-otoshi*.

Throwing action

Very often the *tai-otoshi* leg is scarcely needed; the hands and the total commitment of uke to the *uchimata* are all that is needed.

Tai-otoshi (lifting elbow)

Weight categories

All weights.

Grips

Lapel and sleeve.

Opportunity

Tradition dictates that a lifted elbow is weak, but it need not be so. Sometimes, uke's control of tori's sleeve is so strong that it is impossible to pull. Tori can negate the defence by lifting his elbow sharply.

Entry

This not only raises uke slightly, but equally importantly clears a passage for tori to make his entry.

Tip

This has been illustrated with *Tai-otoshi*, but it works just as well with other throws such as *Uchimata* or *Harai-goshi*.

Hikki-otoshi
(Pulling drop throw)

Weight categories

All weights.

Grips

Middle lapel, sleeve.

Opportunity

The best chance occurs when uke is moving in a half-circle and tori can catch his opponent 'on the hop', so-to-speak. But it is also possible to work this throw from a static position, providing tori achieves a good turn – with a fast action.

Entry

Tori does not just drop on his knee, but aims for some rotation before the knee touches the floor. The sudden drop of his weight must bring uke forward on to the blocking leg, which should be as straight as possible.

Throwing action

This is finally achieved by the hands.

Olympic Light-heavyweight Champion Robert van de Walle (Belgium) catches Britain's Paul Radburn totally by surprise by suddenly dropping to his right knee.

UCHIMATA

Uchimata (direct attack)
(Inner thigh)

Weight categories

All weights.

Grips

Sleeve and high collar.

Entries

Two main entries are used for this kind of power *Uchimata*:

1. Tori hops in on his standing leg and lifts his opponent as high as possible with his other leg.
2. Tori places his lifting leg on the mat between uke's legs, thus placing tori in a sideways stance. Tori swings the other leg backwards. This becomes the supporting leg, allowing the lifting leg to attack strongly. The actual point of attack can be the top of tori's thigh or even the hip.

Direction of throw

Once the lift has been achieved, it is important to control the rotation of the opponent with the sleeve grip.

Roy Inman (opposite) and European Silver Medallist Densign White (Great Britain) (overleaf) showing the lifting action from the leg which is vital in Uchimata.

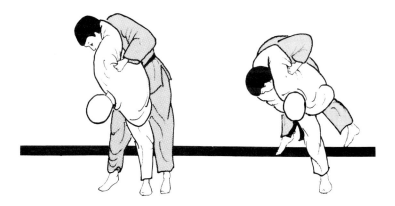

Osoto-gake to Uchimata
(Major outer hook to inner thigh)

Weight categories

All weights.

Grips

High lapel, low sleeve.

Entry

This can be done as a spontaneous follow-on technique. The *Osoto-gake* fails because uke withdraws his attacked leg too far for tori to hook on to. But this wide stance puts uke in a vulnerable posture, and there is often time for tori to hop in to attack with *Uchimata*.

Tip

Tori's attacking leg should not need to touch the ground once the initial *Osoto-gake* attack has been made.

Ouchi-gari into Uchimata
(Major inner reap into inner thigh)

Weight categories

All weights.

Grips

High lapel, low sleeve.

Opportunity

Contestants need to have opposite grips, right against left, with tori having the inside high lapel grip. A testing *Ouchi-gari* finds that tori's opponent is pushing forward slightly.

Entry

Tori pulls on the sleeve grip, bringing uke on to the advanced leg. Immediately, tori picks up the other foot in an *Ouchi-gari* movement. At the same time, his high lapel grip pushes into the side of uke's head, forcing it down, a movement encouraged by a further pull on the sleeve grip. Uke's head must be bent quite low for the throw to work.

Throwing action

This begins with tori hopping towards the back corner, putting uke increasingly on to the side of the advanced foot. Eventually, he can no longer hold out, and must go over for the *Uchimata*.

Tip

The secret of the throw lies in the push-pull action between the lapel and sleeve grips, and the direction of the hop towards the back corner.

Yamashita (opposite) throws with the Ouchi *and* Uchimata *that he made so much his own.*

ASHIWAZA

De-ashi-barai
(**Advanced foot sweep**)

Weight categories

All weights.

Opportunity

This generally comes from a moving situation, when uke is moving away or going sideways.

Tip

With the traditional sleeve and collar grip, tori can theoretically sweep his opponent either to the left or right. Nevertheless, experience shows that he generally sweeps his opponent on the side of the lapel grip, probably because his attacking foot is partially shielded from uke's sight by the grips. There is also a surprise element in this 'wrong side' foot sweep, because traditionally *De-ashi-barai* is taught with the attack against the leg on the same side as the sleeve grip.

White (Great Britain) sweeps Fegert (West Germany) into the air with De-ashi-barai *at the 1986 European Championships, Belgrade.*

Sasae-tsuri-komi-ashi (wrong way)
(Propping drawing ankle)

Introduction

We call this 'wrong way' because traditionally this technique is done by attacking the foot on the same side as the sleeve grip. Attacking the other side adds a strong element of surprise, although sometimes uke can get his hand down to the mat to nullify or lessen the score.

Weight categories

All weights.

Grips

Low sleeve, high collar.

Opportunity

Uke must be positioned slightly off centre, with the leg to be attacked (the same side as tori's lapel grip) further away.

Attacking action

The high collar grip controls uke's head and pulls uke's weight on to his foot. The sole of tori's foot blocks uke's leg in front of the ankle. The rotation now begins, with the high collar grip pulling strongly, aided by the sleeve grip pushing uke's elbow high into the air.

Throwing action

A complete commitment to the rotation is important, with tori following uke down to the mat.

(a)

(c)

(b)

Three examples of effective Tsuri-komi-ashi *done the 'wrong' way, on the lapel grip side.*

Hiza-guruma
(Knee wheel)

Weight categories

All weights.

Grips

Lapel, sleeve, or back of jacket, sleeve.

Opportunity

A *Hiza-guruma* can often be used effectively against a defensive, static opponent with a developed strong-arm defence.

Entry

If the right foot is being used as the blocking leg, the *Hiza-guruma* movement starts with a committed, substantial step with the left leg in the opposite direction to the attack. This creates the optimum position for the attack and ensures that the blocking leg, when it is placed on uke's knee, is straight. It also helps to put most of uke's weight on the leg to be attacked.

Throwing action

The strong wheeling feeling of the throw comes from a good turn of the head in the direction of the throw, followed by a strong twist from uke's upper body and hips.

The classic Hiza-guruma *position, demonstrated by Olympic Heavyweight Bronze Medallist Arthur Mapp (Great Britain).*

KOSOTO-GARI/GAKE

Kosoto-gari
(Minor outer reap)

Olympic Light-middleweight Champion Frank Wieneke (West Germany) (opposite) executes a powerful Kosoto-gari *on his way to winning the European title in 1986.*

Weight categories

All weights.

Grips

The important factor is the control of uke's arm on the side he is attacked. This can be achieved in two ways: holding the outside of the jacket to trap the arm as the photograph shows; or holding the sleeve and pushing the elbow down and across at the time of the attack as the drawings show.

Entry

This is a big lunge action. The lunge action is normally a distinctive feature of a *Gake* throw, but it can generate immense power for a classic reaping action as the photograph shows.

Tip

The attack should be made when tori is square on to uke. The golden rule remains: never attack an advanced foot on the outside unless uke's weight has been brought sharply on to that advanced foot, planting it firmly on the ground. Tori must also have good control of the upper body.

71

Kosoto-gari (the twitch)

Weight categories

All weights.

Grips

Sleeve and lapel or double lapel, but particularly effective with double lapel as this gives tori greater control of uke's chest area.

Opportunity

Uke himself creates the opportunity by blocking a forward throw such as *Uchimata* with a forceful movement of his hips.

Entry

Feint an *Uchimata* or similar forward technique and, as uke blocks, take *Kosoto* to the rear.

Throwing action

It is possible to take just one leg or, even more effectively, both to make it *Nidan-kosoto-gari*.

Comment

I call this the 'twitch' because the feint can be just a slight flick movement of the hips. Often, in the heat of contest, this is enough to make uke over-react.

(a)

(b)

Action and reaction – the end result of 'the twitch': (a) Wieneke (West Germany) and (b) Tripet (France) have made their opponents defend so strongly against a forward throw that the sudden change backwards has produced a levelling effect.

Nidan-kosoto-gari
(Two-leg outer minor reap)

Weight categories

Middle and below, but heavyweights also (*see* Throwing action).

Grips

Normally, lapel and sleeve, but it can also work, as the photograph shows, with double lapel.

Attack

Often an opponent attempts to avoid a *Kosoto-gari* by lifting the threatened leg, and stabilising on the other leg. It comes as quite a surprise to feel a follow-on attack on the standing leg, and often he is so unstable that little more than a touch is necessary to send him toppling over.

Throwing action

However, to make certain of success, many of these *Nidan-kosoto-garis* seen in contest are taken down to the ground in an action closely resembling a *Tani-otoshi*. This applies particularly to heavyweights.

Yuri Sokolov (USSR) wins the 1986 European featherweight title with the Nidan-kosoto-gari.

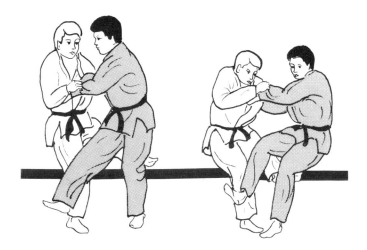

Kosoto-gake (direct attack)
(Minor outer hook)

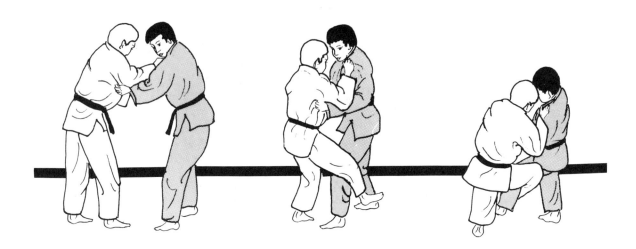

Weight categories

All weights.

Grips

High lapel, low sleeve, or back of jacket and low sleeve.

Entry

Tori attacks either with a lunge or in *Tsugi-ashi* fashion. At the same time, he pulls uke's weight well on to the attacked foot.

Throwing action

The hook often takes uke's foot off the ground, but it is the strong and committed pulling action (aided in the photograph by a sacrifice drop) which finishes the throw.

The total commitment of weight enables this Kosoto-gake *to score.*

Kosoto-gake (one hand)
(Minor outer hook)

Introduction

This may have evolved as a follow-on to the *Kouchi* pick-up which has become quite common.

Weight categories

Middleweights and below.

Grips

Cross grip.

Opportunity

This must be attempted before the players have settled into a head-to-head stance. The opponent must not be able to control thrower's head.

Entry

Tori makes a half-circle step towards the cross grip as if he is going to do the *Kouchi-gari* pick-up. Uke senses this and immediately withdraws the threatened foot, but he is caught by the outer hook.

Kerrith Brown (Great Britain) throws Steffen Stranz (West Germany)
with Kosoto-gake *to reach the lightweight final of the 1986 European*
Championships.

KOUCHI-GARI/GAKE

Kouchi-gari (wrong leg)
(Minor inner reap)

Weight categories

All weights.

Grips

Lapel, sleeve.

Principle

Total surprise – a left-handed throw from a right-handed grip.

Entry

It helps to set up the throw by attacking uke with a conventional *Kouchi-gari* or two. Suddenly reverse the feet action, so that the *Kouchi* attack comes on the other side. Uke's own defence for the first attacks aids the real *Kouchi-gari* attempt on the other side.

Tip

The correct direction of the sweeping foot can be helped by imagining that the sweep will make uke do the splits.

The surprise of a Kouchi-gari *attack on the other side can produce startling results, as here when Japan's Nakahara threw Poland's Majdan on her way to winning a bronze medal in the 1982 Women's World Championships.*

Morote-seoi-nage into Kouchi-gari
(Double hand shoulder throw into minor inner reap)

Weight categories

Middleweights and below.

Grips

Middle lapel and low sleeve.

Entry

Normal entry into *Morote-seoi*, except that the elbow must not tuck under uke's arm, but come over. Tori over-rotates with the hips, so that he is facing the way he came. He can then attack with *Kouchi-gari* or *Kouchi-gake*.

Throwing action

Extra impetus is gained by the total commitment into the throwing action of tori's body-weight.

Tip

This action should be specifically trained for, not regarded just as a spontaneous follow-through in a sudden over-rotation situation.

Iwata (Japan) changes swiftly from a right Seoi-nage *attack to left*
Kouchi-gari *to use his opponent's defensive pull.*

Ippon-seoi-nage into Kouchi-gari
(One-arm shoulder throw into minor inner reap)

Weight categories

Middleweights and below.

Grips

Preferably low sleeve grip, although it can work with lapel grip.

Entry

Tori must convince uke that the *Ippon-seoi* attack is genuine, forcing him to defend by pulling backwards. Nevertheless, tori must not commit his weight from the waist down, but just start to rotate the shoulders.

Throwing action

This enables tori to turn the shoulders again and attack with *Kouchi-gari*.

Austria's Edith Hrovath has not quite succeeded with this Kouchi-gari from the initial Ippon-seoi-nage attack, but the intention is clear.

Uchimata to Kouchi-gari
(Inner thigh to minor inner reap)

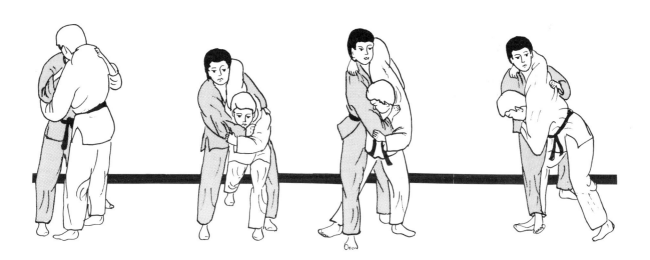

Weight categories

All weights.

Grips

Collar, low sleeve.

Entry

This can work as a spontaneous follow-on combination, but it operates best when tori is actually intending to throw with the *Kouchi-gari* itself. Having already made a strong *Uchimata* attempt which has failed, tori turns in fast with an *Uchimata* action, but keeps a slight gap between himself and uke. This enables him to turn unimpeded into the *Kouchi* attack.

Throwing action

As in most *Kouchi-gari* attacks, the direction of the sweep has to be clear – either taking uke's foot to the side (making uke do a 'splits' action) which requires less hand action; or to sweep the foot more or less in the direction of uke's toes, which requires a strong pinning control with the hands.

Tip

This combination only works when uke is sufficiently worried about the *Uchimata* to block strongly against any suggestion of an attack.

URANAGE

Uranage (classic)
(Rear throw)

Introduction

This is the classic counter throw. It can be done spontaneously but often tori sets a trap.

Weight categories

All weights.

Opportunity

Tori awaits a strong forward attack by uke, with one arm ready to wrap around uke's body.

Counter action

Once uke has committed himself to the attack, tori pulls his opponent's body to him and lifts strongly. He rotates to throw, and adds extra power to the movement with a committed sacrifice.

(a)

(b)

The powerful lift finished by the characteristic twist of the classic
Uranage *by (a) Olympic Heavyweight Champion Angelo Parisi and*
(b) Jean-Pierre Besse (France).

Uranage (front attacking style)

(a)

(b)

The powerful lifting knee makes Uranage *possible from a face-to-face situation, as demonstrated here by (a) Chochosvilli (USSR) and (b) Steffen Stranz (West Germany).*

Introduction

Uranage is generally regarded as a counter, but with slight modifications the principle of throwing to tori's rear can be used as a direct attack from the front. This is a typical example of the influence of other wrestling styles on judo, from sumo to sambo.

Weight categories

Middleweights and above.

Grips

Middle lapel and/or middle of back, or top of thigh and middle of back.

Entry

Tori takes a fast step forward and achieves good control of uke's body by firm body contact. He starts to lean back. Tori brings uke up on his toes, and aids the lift by bringing his knee up. Uke should now be airborne.

Direction of throw

Tori then rotates strongly, pulling uke round.

Uranage (lifting knee counter)

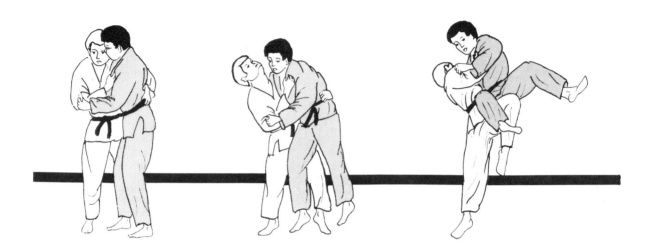

Counter action

Much the same action, but tori assists with the lift by raising the knee against uke's buttocks or top of thigh. This can add considerably to the height of the lift, thus making the rotation more effective and the throw more forceful.

Uranage *counters by (a) Olympic Light-heavyweight Champion Chochosvilli (USSR) and (b) Maurel (France).*

(a)

90

(b)

Uranage combination with hip throw

(a)

(b)

Bodavelli (USSR) produces a superb lifting-knee counter from an apparently unpromising situation. He hooks in as his opponent picks him up, and stabilises with the trouser grip. He then suddenly changes the whole direction of the fight utilising his strong belt grip.

(c)

Weight categories

Middleweights and above.

Opportunity

Tori attacks with *Tsuri-goshi* which is blocked strongly by his opponent. Uke attempts to counter with *Te-guruma,* but tori hooks in.

Preparation

Tori stabilises momentarily with the belt grip then takes the trousers in the other hand. At this point, uke feels that the hooking leg threatens an *Ouchi-gari* attempt.

Throwing action

Tori begins to rotate towards uke, pulling strongly on the belt and beginning to lift with the trouser grip. He aids the whole lifting action by raising the hooking leg, lifting his opponent off the ground. Now, turning his head in the direction of the throw, he must rotate with maximum effort.

Completion

Uke can put his hand down to the mat to lessen the score. Therefore, in order to obtain ippon tori must ensure that the lift is high and that he commits himself completely to the rotation, following uke right down to the ground.

KOSHIWAZA

Oguruma
(Major wheel)

Weight categories

Middleweights.

Grips

Low sleeve, high collar; or double lapel which makes the move unpredictable and allows a strong body pull.

Opportunity

Opponent is moving in a half-circle.

Entry

Tori spins in the same direction as uke is moving, and blocks with the leg on or above the knee.

Throwing action

There is very little lift from the blocking leg. The throwing action comes from the arms, pivoting the opponent over the leg and hips.

Tip

It is important that tori's head turns well, for this allows the body to achieve greater rotation power.

A textbook Oguruma *attack and throwing action from Dawn Netherwood (Great Britain) in the 1986 European Championships.*

Hane-goshi (trouser grip)
(Spring hip)

Weight categories

Middleweights and above.

Grips

Trousers, at the top of the thigh, sleeve.

Entry

Step across, rather than step in as is the traditional fashion. The trouser grip, just below the buttocks, provides a powerful and (for uke) an unexpected lift.

Paul Radburn (Great Britain) surprises his opponent with the unorthodox hand grip just beneath the buttock.

Hane-goshi

Roy Inman scoring with Hane-goshi.

The Japanese World Champion Sumio Endo in classic Hane-goshi
position in the Paris Multi-Nations in 1974.

Introduction

Hane-goshi has rarely been seen in top competition in the last few years, but there are signs that it is returning. It could be argued that many *Uchimatas* seen nowadays are, in reality, very close to *Hane-goshi*.

Weight categories

All weights.

Grips

High collar, low sleeve.

Principle

The objective of *Hane-goshi* is to create a platform with the bent leg which can lift uke.

Opportunity

This works best on an uke who is stepping backwards, yet standing fairly upright.

Entry

In a right-handed throw, tori's left foot follows uke's retreating right foot, and then he pivots in to the attack.

Throwing action

Once uke is airborne, it is not as difficult to rotate him as in *Uchimata*.

Ogoshi
(Major hip throw)

Weight categories

Light heavyweights and above.

Grips

Back of jacket or belt, middle lapel.

Opportunity

It works best against a fairly upright posture.

Entry

Traditional entry is for tori to step in towards opponent, but it is best to step in front so that, using the powerful back grip, uke can be pulled forwards on to tori's hip. This pulling action provides the impetus for the throw; in this version of *Ogoshi* there is very little lift or 'jacking-up' action with the legs.

(a)

(b)

Two examples of the effectiveness of Ogoshi *in competition.*

Tsuri-goshi
(Lift hip)

Weight categories

Middleweights and above.

Grips

One hand holds sleeve or middle lapel.

Entry

Tori prepares for the throw by standing with his right leg advanced (in a right-handed throw) and reaches over swiftly to take the belt. (This should be done with speed and commitment – a casual movement invites a counter.) Tori's back leg then swings in, allowing tori's hips to rotate and place him in position for the throw.

Throwing action

Tori falls forward slightly to pull uke off balance and then rotates strongly to throw, maintaining all the time a strong pull on the belt. The turning and falling action makes the throw feel like a *Makikomi* technique.

The British heavyweight Heather Ford (opposite) attacks with Tsuri-goshi *in the 1982 World Championships.*

Harai-goshi (step away)
(Sweeping hip)

Introduction

The distance needed to be covered by tori for *Harai-goshi* has made it a relatively rare throw in top competition as a direct attack, although it is effectively used with various combinations such as *Uchimata* into *Harai-goshi* or *Ouchi-gari* into *Harai-goshi*. However, it can still be used with good results by stepping away to make the attack, rather than stepping in, which is more easily blocked.

Weight categories

All weights.

Grips

High collar, sleeve.

A superb Harai-goshi *by Guy Auffray (France) from a sleeve/lapel grip. Note trapped arm of uke.*

Entry

In a right-handed attack, tori steps back on his left foot and vigorously draws uke off balance towards him, then brings the sweeping leg across and throws.

MAKIKOMI

Makikomi
(Inner winding)

Introduction

Makikomi is a much maligned throw, one that is often regarded as second best to a pure throw. But this need not be the case: it can work spectacularly when well done.

Weight categories

All weights, but predominantly heavyweights.

Grips

Initially, middle lapel and low sleeve. On attack, lapel grip changes to over opponent's leading arm.

Opportunity

Makikomi seems to work best as a combination – when tori has attacked with a hip throw of some sort and it has been blocked.

Entry

Tori steps in, wraps sleeve grip around his chest, gains good body contact, pushing hips through, and, letting go of his lapel grip, clamps on to uke's leading arm with a forceful action.

(a)

(b)

(c)

The importance of full rotation before tori hits the ground is seen here.

Body movement

Tori must fall forward before he starts to rotate, for the sudden forward movement brings uke off balance.

Throwing action

Now tori can begin the throwing action, winding strongly. The aim should be complete rotation, so that tori ends up facing the ceiling in a hold – only possible if the head is turned well.

107

Makikomi (power curve)
(Inner winding)

Introduction

A similar action, except for different use of rotating arm.

Entry/grips

Instead of clamping on the arm, a well-controlled sleeve grip allows tori to use his lapel-grip arm to form a power curve indicator which leads the whole throw through the circle. This is probably more relevant to lighter weights generating greater speed in their rotation rather than power.

Tip

Decide which one is preferable. Very often, a failed *Makikomi* is one that has fallen somewhere between these two techniques.

European Champion Alexander van der Groeben (West Germany) scores ippon with Harai-makikomi *in the 1986 British Open Championships.*

Osoto-gake to Osoto-makikomi
(Major outer hook to major outer winding throw)

Weight categories

All weights.

Grip

Sleeve grip.

Entry

The entry is similar to the *Osoto-gake*. However, if the initial *gake* attack is not strong, uke can defend by leaning forward. At this point, tori can change direction by changing to the classic winding throw. He will probably not have been able to clamp on uke's arm with his free hand, so he can use the arm to describe a clear power curve which will direct the whole impetus of the throw.

Throwing action

As with all winding throws, tori's hips must be thrown with total commitment into the circle action.

SEOI-NAGE

Morote-seoi-nage on one knee
(Double hand shoulder throw)

Weight categories

Middleweights and below.

Grips

Middle lapel, low sleeve.

Opportunity

This arises when tori finds it impossible to get sufficiently across uke for an orthodox *Seoi-nage* movement – a common contest situation.

Entry

Step across, aiming for the middle of uke's stance. Rotate, pushing elbow under uke's armpit. Drop on one knee.

Direction of throw

Aim to throw to the side, rather than over the top.

Tip

The feeling of the throw is uke's body being pivoted over tori's outstretched hip. It works well when both players are moving sideways at speed.

Two Japanese World Champions score ippon with Seoi-otoshi, *(a) Minami in 1973 and (b) Katsuki in 1978.*

110

(a)

(b)

Eri-seoi-nage (two hands on one lapel)
(Lapel shoulder throw)

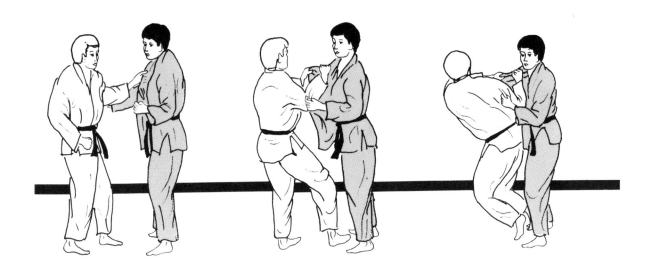

Weight categories

All weights.

Grip

One lapel.

Entry

Tori takes the lapel inside uke's arm, enabling space to be created for the main attack. His other hand grips on the same lapel, just above the right hand (in a left-handed technique), and he steps across, bringing his elbow through in a *Morote-seoi-nage* movement and bringing his hips well through.

Tip

This whole action takes place well before both players have settled down to a static grip situation. It comes from a loose play.

The British heavyweight Paul Radburn uses Eri-seoi-nage *with
spectacular results in the 1978 British Open Championships.*

Drop Eri-seoi-nage
(Lapel shoulder throw)

Weight categories

All weights.

Grips

Cross grip, low sleeve.

Entry

Step across, swinging the back leg in a half-circle, keeping hips well in line with feet. Elbow goes underneath uke's armpit. Once in position, rotate for the throw.

Tip

The cross grip allows plenty of room for the hips to come through and a good rotation to be achieved. Tori must make the most of it.

Japan's middleweight Chinen attacks Bielawski (Poland) with Drop Eri-seoi-nage.

Drop Morote-seoi-nage (elbow outside)
(Double-arm shoulder throw)

Weight categories

Middleweights and below.

Grips

Standard lapel and sleeve grip.

Principle

The same principle is used as in the *Sode-tsuri;* the action of taking the elbow outside comes as a complete surprise to the opponent, who doesn't feel it is very threatening – until it is too late.

Entry

The normal entry for *Morote-seoi-nage* involves tori bringing the elbow towards uke and across his body – a relatively easy movement to stop. But this elbow outside version is done by tori bringing his elbow slightly away from uke in order to bring it over the arm and clamp on.

Throwing action

The feeling of the throw is closer to a *Makikomi* in the sense of the exaggerated rotation than a *Seoi-nage*.

Loretta Doyle (Great Britain) attacks with an unorthodox elbow outside Seoi-nage *on her way to winning her world featherweight title in Paris, 1982.*

Ippon-seoi-nage
(One arm shoulder throw)

Introduction

It seems that the standard form of *Ippon-seoi-nage* operated by a sleeve grip is very difficult in modern judo, unless there is a great disparity of skill between contestants. The lapel grip provides the tight body contact that the throw requires.

Weight categories

Middleweights and below.

Grip

Lapel grip over opponent's arm.

Entry

The most common entry for *Ippon-seoi-nage* is the step-across, but it has to be done before uke has settled in to a grip.

Tips

The use of the hips, coming well through, is crucial to the success of the throw in its standing form.

Hidetoshi Nakanishi (Japan) uses his powerful Ippon-seoi-nage *from a standing position at the Paris Multi-Nations, 1982.*

Drop Seoi-nage
(Shoulder throw)

(a)   *(b)*

Britain's Lightweight Champion Ann Hughes with Light-middleweight Champion Diane Bell demonstrates (a) Drop Morote-seoi and (b) Drop Ippon-seoi.

Neil Adams attacks with Drop Ippon-seoi-nage.

Weight categories

All weights.

Grips

Middle lapel, sleeve.

Principle

As in most 'dropped' throws, the sudden fall of tori's bodyweight should work in exactly the same way as the standard sacrifice throw, such as a *Tomoe-nage*.

Entry

The turn into the throw is a half-spin, with, in the case of the right-handed throw, the left leg reaching its final position in between uke's legs as the drop begins.

Throwing action

Tori takes uke over the top or to the side, depending on the position.

Tip

It is necessary to study and practise the drop carefully. If tori drops too early, he does not achieve sufficient turn. If he drops too late, the element of surprise is lost, and uke can come off the throw. Only when the spin and drop are correct does the throw work well. Otherwise, it becomes just a purposeless flop and drop.

Drop Ippon-seoi-nage does not seem to be as popular as the dropped form of *Morote-seoi-nage*.

121

Drop Sode-tsuri-komi-goshi (elbow outside)
(Sleeve-pull hip throw)

(a)

(b)

Liezy Nakani (USSR) gained a waza-ari for this Drop Sode-tsuri-komi-goshi *against Istvan Nagy (Romania) in the 1986 European Championships.*

Weight categories

Middleweights and below.

Grips

Ideally two sleeves, although it works well with sleeve and lapel.

Opportunity

This throw generally comes from a static position, for it is the surprise element of turning in the unexpected direction that breaks the defence.

Entry

In a traditional *Sode-tsuri-komi-goshi* the arm is pushed up and the hips rotate underneath. In this one, because of the strength of uke's defence, tori cannot lift uke's sleeve very high. But it is raised just high enough for tori to get his elbow across and over uke's forearm, on to which he then clamps. This clamping action brings uke firmly on to tori's back, and uke's normal reaction is to attempt to resist.

Throwing action

It is at this point that tori drops swiftly to his knees, breaking uke's balance. Tori drives up off his knees and, with a strong rotation, takes the opponent on to his back.

(c)

Seoi-otoshi
(Shoulder drop)

Weight categories

All weights.

Grips

Double lapel.

Entry

Tori stands slightly off centre and swivels into the attack, with the attacking leg going past

uke's far leg at above knee height. Tori plants the foot on the ground and gains a strong base. His hips then come firmly through with the elbow coming across the chest and under the opposite lapel. This gives tori's elbow a base to lift and pull from. To achieve this gap for the elbow it is important to pull the other lapel thereby creating space.

Comment

One of the most spectacular throws of all. It is worth noting that the two photographs, showing the same attacker, were taken with four years in between – yet the action is exactly the same.

France's Olympic Heavyweight Champion Angelo Parisi at (a) the British Open, 1973, and (b) Paris Multi-Nations, 1977.

(a) *(b)*

TOMOE-NAGE

Tomoe-nage (classic)
(Stomach throw)

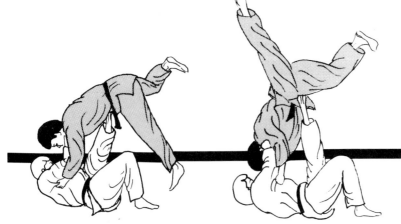

Weight categories

All weights.

Grips

Lapel, sleeve.

Principle

The popular concept of *Tomoe-nage* is as a circle throw, with uke forming one half of the circle and tori the other half.

Opportunity

This is signalled by a bent posture from uke, pushing slightly forwards. The precise cue for timing is when uke steps forward on his right leg (for a right-handed throw). Tori must step in with his left foot before placing his right foot just above uke's belt.

Problems

While it does still work (as the photograph shows) in top competition, this form of *Tomoe-nage* means uke spends a fair time in the air, enabling most players with even basic gymnastic skills to spin out of the throw. This is why other forms of *Tomoe-nage*, such as *Yoko-tomoe-nage* developed.

Roy Inman throws with classic Tomoe-nage.

Tomoe-nage (somersault style)

Weight categories

Middleweights and below.

Grips

Double lapel or lapel and sleeve.

Opportunity

It works best against a fairly upright posture with a wide stance, with uke pushing slightly.

Entry

The feel of the entry is akin to a backward somersault. Tori does not just drop to the ground. On the contrary, he jumps into the air, placing one foot high into uke's stomach area. The sudden weight pulls uke forward. As tori falls towards the mat, he swings his backside as far between uke's legs as possible. It is important that tori's other leg swings up under uke's armpit, for this forces tori to commit himself entirely to a back somersault action. If this attack is done in a faint-hearted

manner, uke can stop the attack and counter simply by banging tori down on to his back.

Direction of throw

The direction is right over the top.

Shozo Fujii (Japan) wins his fourth consecutive world title by throwing Bernard Tchoullouyan (France) with his somersault Tomoe-nage *in 1979.*

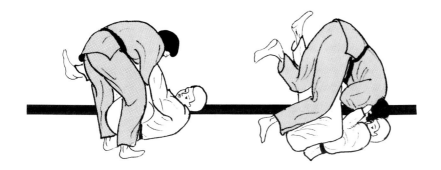

Tomoe-nage (double foot)

Weight categories

Lightweights.

Grips

Invariably double lapel.

Entry

This is similar to the somersault *Tomoe-nage*, except that both feet are placed virtually simultaneously at the front of uke's hips. The purpose of the feet is to control uke's direction like a pair of hands.

Throwing action

This is a strong rotation, generally over the top as in the classic *Tomoe-nage*, although uke can be taken to the sides.

Beatrice Rodriguez (France) throws at the 1981 British Open, with a double-foot Tomoe-nage.

Yoko-tomoe-nage
(Side stomach throw)

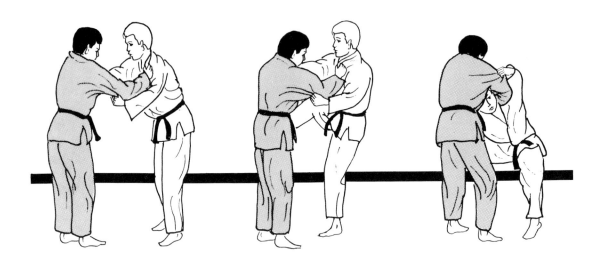

Introduction

There are various kinds of *Tomoe-nage* which involve tori making a side entry to throw his opponent straight over the top or to either side should he try to turn out of the throw. The basic principle of most *Yoko-tomoe-nages* is to throw uke over the sleeve grip.

Weight categories

Middleweights and below.

Grips

Lapel, sleeve or even two sleeves.

Entry

Place foot in opponent's stomach and, on the immediate resistance, twist to the side on falling. Uke's resistance will indicate the direction of the throw.

Karen Briggs on her way to her first world title in Paris, 1982, using her Yoko-tomoe-nage *with full control.*

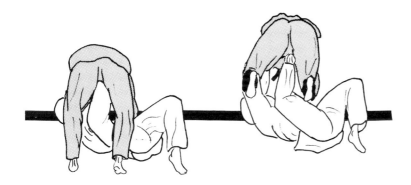

Tomoe-nage with knee block

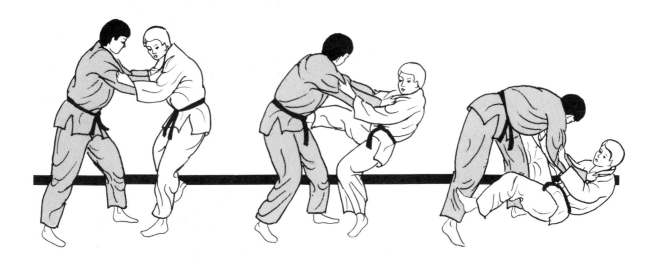

Weight categories

Middleweights and below.

Grips

Middle lapel and sleeve.

Entry

Tori uses a classic *Tomoe-nage* entry, but uke manages to keep his weight slightly back so that tori finds himself on his back with only partial lift from a straight leg. Uke invariably steps forward to brace against the throw.

Throwing action

This is what tori has been waiting for. He places his foot on the knee and, using a blocking or sweeping action, brings his opponent over on to his side.

Tip

If uke has retained only a small amount of control, the sweeping action can result in a high score. If he has retained a fair amount of his balance, the blocking action will bring him down for a smaller score.

Karen Briggs adds a knee block to her Tomoe-nage *to throw Scotland's Anne-Marie Mulholland to win the 1986 Commonwealth Games title.*

MISCELLANEOUS SUTEMI-WAZA

Yoko-gake
(Side hook)

Weight categories

Middleweights and above.

Grips

Most grips.

Opportunity

Best in a square-stance situation, or when uke's leg to be attacked is slightly trailing.

Entry

This is either a fast *Tsugi-ashi* stepping movement, or a lunge. The importance lies in the sudden drop of tori's bodyweight to bring uke's bodyweight sharply on to the attacked leg.

Throwing action

Once the leg is hooked, tori's fall to the side completes the throw.

Direction of throw

Uke should fall directly to the side.

The beginning of a strong Yoko-gake *by Maurel (France).*

Kani-basami
(Crab pinch)

Introduction

This is sometimes regarded as a dangerous throw because a badly executed technique can damage uke's knees or legs. Judo federations periodically discuss banning it, although at the time of writing it is accepted. There is no doubt, however, that it is an effective throw when well done.

Weight categories

All weights.

Grip

Single lapel grip on the side to be attacked.

Entry

Tori begins with an *Oguruma* action with the leg going across uke's upper thighs. The other leg goes behind the back of the knees, or just above the calf – but no lower, for this is when the injuries occur.

Throwing action

The break of balance comes partly by tori pulling uke sharply towards him, and partly by the sudden drop of tori's weight. The actual throw comes from the scissor action, aided by tori turning well on to his back after hitting the ground.

138

Jean-Luc Rouge (France) attacks David Starbrook (Great Britain) with
Kani-basami *on his way to winning the European light-heavyweight title*
in Lyons in 1975.

Yoko-wakare
(Side separation)

Weight categories

Middleweights and below.

Grips

Over-arm lapel.

Opportunity

This is a throw that can be spectacular, but needs the ideal starting conditions. Both players must be in relatively bent postures, with uke having what appears to be the dominant grip – for example, a strong right arm over tori's shoulder, forcing tori's head down.

Entry

Holding firmly on to the over-arm lapel grip, tori's other arm attacks as if for *Ippon-seoi-nage*, but at the same time his leg comes swiftly through. As his body falls towards the ground, tori rotates so that he falls on to his side and stomach.

Throwing action

This totally committed fall and spin creates a powerful centrifugal force which is unleashed as uke is taken over the top and down to the mat.

Tip

The success of the throw relies on the tight grip of both hands and the fast and committed spin.

World Lightweight Champion Ann Hughes (Great Britain) demonstrates
Yoko-wakare.

Sumi-gaeshi (one arm)
(Corner throw)

Weight categories

All weights.

Grips

Lapel, sleeve on the same side. From standard sleeve, lapel grip, tori lets go of sleeve grip with left hand (in a right-handed throw) and picks up uke's left sleeve. If possible, tori then breaks uke's grip on his lapel and, with his right hand, takes a grip deep at the back of uke's jacket, or even on the belt.

Entry

Tori can then feint for a kind of *Ogoshi* or *Uchimata* throw before stepping in with the left foot and hooking with his right leg behind uke's right inner thigh, or, if uke is already pulling backwards, he can step in and hook straight away.

Throwing action

Most of the work is done by the right hand on the back of the jacket, but tori must maintain strong body contact all through the technique.

Tip

This is often used as a take-down technique, for it offers good immediate groundwork control.

Uki-waza
(Floating throw)

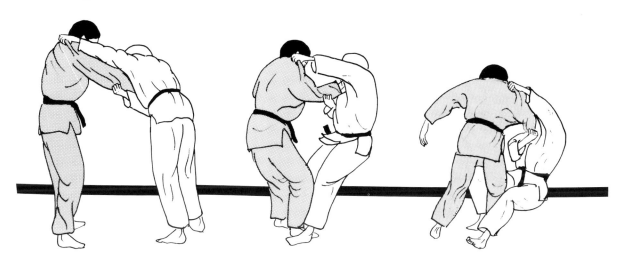

Weight categories

All weights.

Grips

Low sleeve, high collar or back of jacket on the same side.

Opportunity

This works well in conjunction with the *Sumi-gaeshi* from the same grip, but before the opponent has developed a strong, static defence.

Entry

The initial attack is similar to a classic *Hiza-guruma* entry, with tori stepping boldly in front of his opponent in a half-circle action. It is this movement that brings uke on to his forward foot, creating the throw.

Throwing action

Tori commits his body totally to the sacrifice, while at the same time blocking uke's foot with his outstretched leg and turning well into the throw.

Tip

This throw depends on two elements: total surprise and a bold almost flamboyant attack.

Sumi-gaeshi
(Corner throw)

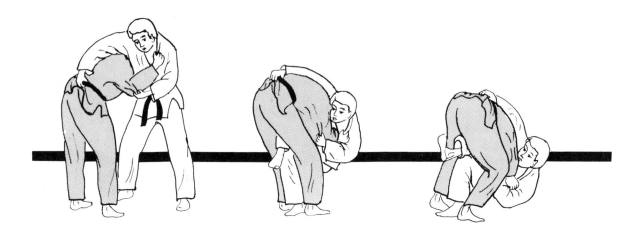

Weight categories

Middleweights and below.

Grips

Belt and sleeve.

Entry

Holding the sleeve grip, tori throws his other arm over uke's shoulder to grab the belt, pressing firmly into uke's back with the elbow to maintain the required bent posture of the opponent. Ensuring close body contact (if possible, controlling uke's head with his armpit), tori hooks into uke's inner thigh, hops a step closer, and sits down on his backside.

Throwing action

Pulling strongly on the belt grip, tori brings uke more or less directly over his head, and does a backward roll, which, ideally, should take him straight into *Tate-shiho-gatame*.

Tips

1. The entry can vary. The step can precede the hook; or, if the opponent is clearly suspecting a *Sumi-gaeshi*, a light *Kouchi-gari* attack from the belt grip can make him push forward slightly in defence, making a smooth *Sumi-gaeshi* more possible.
2. The crucial belt grip can be strengthened by ensuring that the thumb is well tucked into the belt, not just the fingers.

Sumi-gaeshi *from the belt grip — increasingly recognised as a throw in its* *own right rather than just a take-down.*

Waki-otoshi
(Armpit drop)

Weight categories

Middleweights and below.

Grips

Sleeve grip.

Entry

This initially looks like a traditional *Ippon-seoi-nage*, but tori's shoulders only make a feint towards the front throw. The right arm (in a right-handed throw) goes across uke's chest, angled slightly downwards so that the hand ends at about hip level. Meanwhile tori's legs have prepared for the *Tani-otoshi* action.

Throwing action

Uke is caught in a scissor action, with tori's arm pushing over uke's blocked legs.

Tip

To keep the throw tight and controlled it is necessary to pull well on the sleeve grip, for this tori uses a sideways body contact control.

Tani-otoshi (one knee)
(Valley drop)

Weight categories

All weights.

Grips

High lapel, low sleeve or back of jacket and low sleeve.

Entry

Using a *Tsugi-ashi* stepping movement, tori comes to the side and partially behind uke and, with the nearest leg, blocks at the back of uke's knee.

Throwing action

By suddenly sinking his bodyweight, uke begins to tip backwards and unexpectedly meets the blocking leg – which actually causes the throw.

Algisi (France) catches Reissmann (East Germany) with a one-knee Tani-otoshi *at the 1975 European Team Championships.*

TACHIWAZA–NEWAZA

Ude-gatame (applied in tachiwaza)
(Straight armlock)

Introduction

The separation between tachiwaza and newaza is not always clear-cut – in fact, they can be closely interwoven.

Weight categories

Middleweights and above.

Entry

Tori's first move is to step back, creating a gap between himself and uke. At the same time he lets go with both hands and brings his right elbow (in a right-handed attack) over uke's left, outstretched arm. Tori's attacking right arm wraps around uke's arm to the back of the elbow joint, where it is joined by the left hand.

Application

The armlock is achieved by applying the force in an anticlockwise direction. At this point uke often drops to his knees to save the elbow (as the photograph shows) or does a forward roll which creates an opportunity for formal *Juji-gatame*.

Tip

Uke's passage to the ground can be best controlled by tori moving in a small anti-clockwise half-circle.

Neil Adams attacks his defensive opponent with a standing armlock.

Juji-gatame (flying armlock style)

Weight categories

Middleweights and below. (The sequence features a light-heavyweight, which shows just how unpredictable judo can be. But this technique is generally more feasible for lighter weights.)

Grips

Sleeve.

Entry

As the fighters come to grips, tori immediately leaps up into a *Juji-gatame* position from underneath. The sudden weight on uke's arm drags him off balance, straightening the arm at the same time.

Tip

This move requires a real sense of abandon from the moment tori takes hold of uke's sleeve. Any hesitation, and the chance is lost.

(a)

(b)

A superb armlock sequence (a) to (h) initiated from tachiwaza by Valery Divisenko (USSR) who catches the experienced German Gunther Neureuther totally by surprise. Divisenko attacked with it just twenty seconds after the start of the contest in the European Championships 1983, and it brought an immediate submission.

(c)

(d)

(e)

(f)

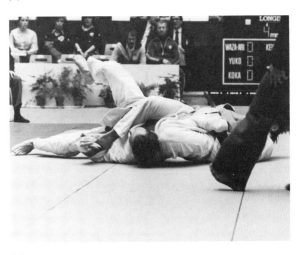

(g)

(h)

3 Developing a Contest Skill

The lack of systematic teaching in judo all too often creates a dabbler's mentality. In most clubs, one part of each judo class is set aside for teaching. Within two or three weeks, a dozen or more techniques involving standing and groundwork can be covered, leaving little time for even a keen individual to establish a skill in any one or two of them. For establishing a judo skill can take time. Sometimes, even serious and diligent work on a new throw will not begin to produce consistent contest results until six months or a year later. It takes time for the individual to absorb the basic movement in his own movement pattern, and to begin to learn to use it against varying defences. Therefore it must be realised that a commitment to develop a throw is a long-term affair, and a decision must not be made lightly.

Here are some guidelines to developing a contest skill:

1. Look at your current major throws, and what they normally score. Look at the minor throws, and what they normally score. Is there an obvious weakness – the lack of a throw to one side or to one angle; the lack of a throw against a particular defence; in extreme circumstances, the lack of a throw against a particular opponent?

2. Decide on a throw that not only suits the situation, but is also likely to suit your own ability, size, and movement pattern. It is probably not worth a man of six foot six inches to adopt *Morote-seoi-nage* as a special study.

3. First of all, consider the basic mechanics.
(a) Look at the ideal grips.
(b) Look at the entries. Which is the quickest and/or most effective entry to bypass, slip, or blast through the opponent's defences – one-step, two-step, jump in, hop in, or pull the opponent's body on to you?
(c) Look at the various options for the direction of the throw.
(d) Which is the ideal stance from which to attack?
(e) Should the opponent be moving or static?
(f) Then begin to work at the *Uchikomi*, first of all standing still and practising the entry, with occasional throws.
(g) Then start to incorporate movement, initially with just a one-step pattern, then gradually introducing variety and covering larger areas of the mat.
(h) After some time has passed the technique should be ready to be introduced into the randori sessions, first of all against lighter and/or less-experienced players.
(i) Only when some fluency has been obtained should you begin to use it against equals.
(j) Gradually, introduce it into contests, first of all in the less-important events.

ADDITIONAL POINTS

Very often a new skill needs time to settle down. This cannot be forced – sometimes it can fail for months and then suddenly appear, as if from nowhere, as a mature contest technique.

A golden rule is to establish real accuracy in the entry and throwing movement right at the beginning. First impressions are very often crucial, so the first impressions made upon the body memory should be the correct ones. Make each aspect of the throw – entry, lift, rotation – precise. You should be very clear of what you are aiming to do at each point in the throw. It is not enough to leap in with a fast and extravagant movement and hope that it will work.

Only when the throw is becoming established should you consider spin-offs from the movement, in terms of other opportunities or combinations. But while working on the throw, begin to consider what counters might be involved. A study of counters to a favourite throw is as important as a study of the throw itself or combinations.

RANDORI

Randori traditionally forms the major part of judo training. Often, however, the emphasis is on quantity rather than quality. Greater emphasis should be placed on quality and more specific work. An ideal breakdown of judo training time is as follows:

Supplementary fitness training: 30 per cent.
Specific judo skills training: 30 per cent.
Randori: 40 per cent.

However, the randori must not generally be a period when anything goes. The object of randori is not to go out and throw as many people as often as possible with your favourite throw. It is important to structure the randori carefully in order to make use of those eight practices, or however many you can get at one session.

It is necessary to keep the established major and minor throws of your repertoire in good condition, and to check for any faults or areas of slackness that may be creeping in. It is also necessary to make space for the new techniques you are trying to develop.

Before the session, you should make a plan. This can consist of anything, from direct attacks to counters, to combinations. You can concentrate on major throws, minor throws, even on being defensive if you are particularly weak in that area. What follows is one suggestion of a randori plan to be used in each practice during the course of one session.

Direct attacks – no combinations. Each attack must be an attempt to score ippon. High collar, low sleeve grip.

1. *Uchimata* (go on to next attack regardless of whether it succeeds or fails).
2. *Sasae-tsuri-komi-ashi* (a throw on the other side).
3. *Ouchi-gari* (a throw to the rear).
4. *Kouchi-gari* (change of the side of attack).
5. *Osoto-gake* (after two inside leg attacks, an outside leg attack).

Then return to number 1. This pattern can be continued more or less regardless of the stance of the opponent or his grips.

By developing a plan such as this, the player puts himself under the control of a structure, leaving less opportunity for the myriad of distractions that randori can offer – the concern of being countered, the desire to level that particular opponent to prove a point, the feeling that it is time to take a little rest, the fear of an opponent and so on. It also cuts out spontaneous actions, though often these will occur in any case when truly spontaneous.

There are an infinite number of permutations for such a randori plan. Even making the plan is a training not only in developing a skill but in tactical work as well. The immense physical demands made by judo upon the individual should not prevent active and creative use being made of brain power.

FITNESS

Many recreational judo players get fit by doing judo. Serious contest players must get fit to a much higher standard in order to do serious contest judo – it is as simple as that. Contrary to the old judo adage, skill levels do not normally improve when a player is tired and can no longer use his muscles effectively. When a player becomes tired his timing goes, his level of co-ordination decreases, and he ceases to think clearly. A fit man, full of energy, can concentrate on his opponent. A tired man, going on the defensive, can only think of himself. A fit man, because he is more physically and mentally alert, is less likely to suffer injuries. A fit man is far more capable of producing the explosive power that is at the heart of so many judo movements.

So the object of fitness in judo is very simple: a judo man must be as fit as possible in order to maintain the skill level as long as possible. For contest purposes that means an ability to do good judo for at the very least six sets of five minutes, which is the number of contests that would take a player to the final in most events. This, of course, could be extended to about eight five-minute randoris, which are generally slightly more relaxed.

The fitness demands made upon the judo player are extreme – there is no doubt about that. The top players tend to be among the fittest in sport generally. There are four areas that must be considered specifically: muscular strength; muscular endurance; cardio-vascular endurance; and flexibility.

Muscular strength

This provides players with a strength base which, when combined with speed, becomes explosive power. It is the main driving force of all judo actions – at least in the contest environment. If a player has no confidence in his muscular condition, he cannot be expected to perform in the tight defensive situation of competition.

Muscular strength also allows the player to control an opponent, so it is vital to defence as well as attack.

Specific training Weight training is the most direct way of improving strength levels. Low repetitions of heavy weights will automatically increase levels of strength. But handling weights is a skill on its own, and a weight training programme should be implemented under the eye of any experienced weights coach.

Muscular endurance

Muscular endurance involves the ability of the player to work continuously – and is very different in quality to muscular strength.

Specific training It is developed by circuit training with high repetitions over sustained periods, such as 30 sit-ups, 30 press-ups, 30 squat thrusts, 30 squat jumps – and then the series repeated as often as the player can reasonably manage.

Relatively long running distances – four to five miles a day – also make an important contribution to the development of muscular endurance.

Cardio-vascular endurance

This is basically the breathing system. A good cardio-vascular system is crucial to the judo player for it gives him a good recovery rate, without which successive bursts of attacking patterns during a five-minute contest are not possible. The body learns to make up the oxygen debt efficiently.

Specific training Fast work – shuttles, sprints, cycling, swimming – all these accustom the body to working well under conditions of intense physical stress.

Flexibility

Perhaps the most widely ignored of the main areas of fitness in judo, but of increasing importance. Increasing the range of movements in all the major joints of the body gives greater opportunities in attack and defence. But flexibility also implies strength in extension – it is not enough to have the flexibility of a rag doll – and flexibility in movement, in terms of gymnastic ability.

Specific training Systematic stretching exercises using all the major joints should be a regular part of all warm-up and warm-down sessions. In addition, trampolining and at least basic gymnastic work is extremely helpful.

MENTAL PREPARATION

The best mental preparation a player can have for contest is his belief that he is as well prepared for the event as he could ever be. He must feel that he is fit, strong, technically equipped to the best of his ability, tactically aware and that he has studied his opponents. If a player has cheated on his training, he will know it.

This is the best guideline for mental preparation. It is also the most difficult, because it involves consistent hard but intelligent work over a considerable period.

Of course, every player, from beginner to champion, suffers nerves before a contest. The shot of adrenalin released by the tension should make the player faster and stronger, but it can also freeze a man's feet to the mat. However, as players gain in experience they generally learn to control nerves.

In addition to this, there is an increasingly popular range of psychological gambits to bring a sportsman to a mental peak. Among these are various visualisation practices, in which the sportsman mentally works his way through a fight against a specific opponent. In this way he can prepare for the possibility of being a koka down with thirty seconds to go, and learn to combat the rising feeling of hopelessness which can often impede positive attacks. He can also condition himself to the reality of beating the unbeatable – often a player can lose not because of his technical ability, but because the form book says so. It is not enough for the coach to point out the unpredictability of judo, with the clash of styles and the possibility that the unbeaten world champion may stub his toe and go over for ippon. That player must believe it in his own mind. The confidence must be an internal one.

It must also be recognised that some players have a determination, a will to win, that is part of the bedrock of their personality. This is something that very often cannot be taught. It is something that transcends physical ability and, occasionally, makes champions of men and women who technically should not be in the medals. This kind of person is often separated from his peers by an ability to perform better when under severe pressure. This kind of person possesses an inner mental drive, a will to win, which, when combined with natural physical talent and the ability to train hard and consistently, makes the outstanding champion. Perhaps this kind of person is born and not made.

But people like this are extremely rare. More often than not, a person has some of those qualities but not all, and the trick is to know the weakness, to control it as much as possible, and compensate for it in some way.

In the end, mental training for contests comes down to the fairly simple business of setting practical goals and being physically, technically, and tactically prepared to achieve them.

4 Contest Tactics

Judo has had an uneasy relationship with tactics. Ever since the established ju-jitsu schools tried to challenge the growing popularity and power of Kodokan judo, by attempting to drag Kano's fighters to the ground in order to win a victory with their superior groundwork, there has been an acute awareness of the use and abuse of tactics. On the one hand, such use of tactics seems to sit uncomfortably with the ethical aims of judo, and yet neither Kano – who eventually disposed of the opposition with the shrewd tactic of creating his own rules – nor his successors could deny their practical use.

Tactics have always played a part in combat, both in attack and defence. A boxer who knows he has not the punch to knock out his opponent has to weave and duck and block – he is not going to drop his gloves, bare his chin, and take it like a man. In much the same way, if a judo player with less natural ability or skill faces a world champion who doesn't like to be pulled around so that he cannot do his technically fine judo, why shouldn't he try to unsettle him by doing just that? After all, a tactic is defined merely as a skilful device to obtain a result. Perhaps a capable use of tactics is as much a developed skill as a good *Tai-otoshi*, and there is little doubt that, in judo, a good tactician can beat a good technician.

There are various kinds of tactics. If a player pulls his opponent sharply, he can generally expect to get a reaction. He can then use that reaction. If he plans the attack, he gives a sharp pull forwards and, as soon as his opponent resists, throws him backwards. This is the basic approach to combinations and is a developed, and highly respectable, judo tactic.

The combination could be extended to cover three attacks, one rapidly following another in order to really unbalance uke.

Alternatively, the same principle can be extended over a longer time-span. At the beginning of the contest tori attacks uke with a forward throw. Twenty seconds later he tries again with a similar attack. On both occasions uke pulls back in defence. After another twenty seconds he attacks a third time, this time with just a feint forward, but changes immediately into a rear throw and the opponent reacts as predicted with the inevitable consequences. This may seem less of a tactic and more of a well-considered if rather elementary attacking plan, but this kind of lively planning is a very necessary part of the contest player's armoury. So are the points that follow.

POSTURE

An acute awareness of posture, both your own and your opponent's, is crucial in judo. Only if you are aware of the implications of certain postures, and the posture requirements of certain throws, particularly your strong throws, can you hope to produce the right throw at the right time.

There are three fundamental postures, but numerous variations of each. The first is the standard upright posture (*see* opposite). Its advantage is that it allows a good range of attacking possibilities because there is more mobility. Its disadvantages are that its defence must rely on the strength of arms, and fast feet, and, of course, it offers the opponent a larger range of attacking opportunities.

(a) Standard upright posture.   *(b) 90 degree posture.*   *(c) 45 degree posture.*

The second is the 90 degree posture (*see* above). This may look like a purely defensive posture, but it is not. Many people have been able to develop good and varied attacking patterns from this bent posture which offers a fair natural defence. However, it does make the player susceptible to forward throws.

The 90 degree posture is not to be confused with what I call the 45 degree posture (*see* above), the third basic posture that is often taken. This is the real defensive posture with its proponent generally locking his arms in defence and sinking his weight on to his heels. It is difficult to attack from here, although some manage it. This posture is very susceptible to rear throws such as *Ouchi-gari* or *Kouchi-gari*.

An experienced player should know immediately which posture he is being faced with, even with one of the many variations, for this will automatically affect his choice of attack. However, sometimes it is difficult for the player to see, and this is where a coach can offer useful comment on the side of the mat.

Players must know their own postures – which they prefer, what their strengths and their weaknesses are – and they should be able to vary their own posture in order to cope with different opponents. If you always like standing upright, and come across an opponent who knows that that is the only

way you can operate, he can frustrate all your attacks simply by pulling your head down. However, every player must have a reasonably strong attack sequence from this bent posture in order to cope with all the eventualities likely to be met on the contest mat.

GRIPS

Most judo players will only attack with their strong techniques once they have got their particular grips. As a rule of thumb, once they have their grips, they will settle for a short time – which can be just a fraction of a second – before launching into the attack. A good example of this is the *Uchimata* specialist who likes a high collar and sleeve grip.

When facing this kind of opponent, the first objective must be to frustrate the grip. Simply fend it off. Try to get your attacks in as he is struggling to get his grip. But, if he is an experienced fighter, don't be surprised if he does get it; if he is persistent, and really needs the grip, he will probably get it during the course of the contest. When he does, don't let him settle with it. Fight to get rid of it. If you can't shake it off, you can forestall his attack by attacking yourself – although this may not score, it will disrupt his rhythm.

An obvious but important point is that all

157

players must have an alternative grip to use with their own major technique. If players cannot work from another grip, they can easily be left stranded by a shrewd tactician.

Grips as a defence

The main defence for most people is the lapel grip. Players feel that if they control the chest and shoulders of their opponent, they are less vulnerable to attack – and to a large extent, they are right. So if you are having difficulty getting past the defences of an opponent, it often pays to look at their lapel grip. Does it need shaking off or nullifying or attacking directly as in a *Sode-tsuri-komi-goshi*, in order to allow some movement? Is your defence controlling your opponent?

ADVANCED FOOT

Another rule of thumb in judo is not to attack the advanced foot from the outside. Most stances in modern judo are at least slightly to one side, with an emphasis on the leading foot. It often looks an inviting target, not least because it is closer. However, it is wise to remember that your opponent is very accustomed to being attacked on that foot and has had ample time to develop strong counter throws with it, and launch attacks from it. Be wary. There is no real reason why it should not be attacked, providing you have ensured that you have controlled your opponent's weight, and it is advisable that you attack it from the inside with a technique such as a *Kouchi-gari*. A strong attack can then surprise even a good defence.

It is also worth remembering that your opponent is probably much weaker on the back leg, his stabilising leg. There is more ground to cover to get to it. But once it has been reached, it often needs surprisingly little force to destabilise the man completely.

PREDICTABILITY

As fighters progress through their contest years, their main techniques become very well known, especially with current video technology. Not only are their techniques analysed, but also their movement patterns, their grips, their likes, dislikes and their weak points. This applies especially to the champions. So it is necessary to change as the years pass, to add new techniques to the old and to try to maintain a strong element of unpredictability in contest work. This does not necessarily mean producing new and strong major throws each year – which is very difficult in judo. But it is possible to introduce small techniques to hide the entry of the old favourites. Top players have to learn to use different grips, perhaps attack on a different side. More contests are lost through predictability as fighters get older than through the effects of time on speed or fitness.

RED LINE

The rules are there to be used, so use them. This means using the red line if you feel it is an advantage. Often, a fighter who constantly takes the gripping battle to the red line before launching an attack is signalling his lack of confidence in his groundwork. But intelligent use of the red line can be a legitimate tactic; whether it is encouraging an opponent to step forward on to a throw in order to avoid stepping out and incurring a penalty, or if you are tired and need a short respite from the constant pressure to which you are being subjected – you can engineer a 'matte' call.

It is worth remembering that many players are slightly distracted by the possibility of incurring a penalty when near the red line, which is why more attacks are launched in this area of the mat.

If you do play the red line, however, you must be prepared to pay the consequences of penalties should you make a mistake.

RULES

All contest players should be familiar with the rules and their current interpretation. This applies especially to the interpretation of passivity and to all actions which can result in penalties, such as illegal throws, grips, and use of the red line.

DEFENCE TACTICS

It is important for players to know when their opponents are being tactically defensive. Are they waiting for you to attack, or are they just sitting back on a koka waiting for the time to tick away? Also, players must be able to make defensive attacks which look as if they are strong but which, in reality, do not involve real commitment.

FIRST ATTACK

Often, the fighter who puts in the first strong attack will be able to dominate, at least for the initial part of the contest. Even if that first attack doesn't score, it means that one man is taking the initiative while the other is on the defensive, and a pattern is being set. However, if you do attack first, make sure it is a strong attack. First attacks can often be hindered by nerves – and such hesitant attacks are easily countered.

Incidentally, if you are scored against, your opponent is often occupied with momentary self-congratulation – leaving you with a good opportunity to attack.

TACTICAL CONFUSION

It helps to try and avoid setting easily readable patterns of behaviour. If a player starts a contest with an upright stance, takes a relatively relaxed grip, and moves smoothly, it is surprising how often an opponent will

follow. Whereas, if the player had steamed in from the start, a strong defence would automatically have been formed by the opponent.

If, in such a contest, the player changes half-way through and begins to fight and maul, tearing grips, bending over, and, after a minute or so, returns to an upright posture, he can end up with a totally confused opponent who is easily throwable.

THROWS TO THE OPPOSITE SIDE

All players must be able to throw to the opposite side of the prevailing grip. If a player generally works from a right-handed sleeve and collar grip, he must be able to work at least one left-handed throw from that position – such as left *Sasae-tsuri-komi-ashi* (wrong way version), left *Ippon-seoi-nage*, left *Kata-guruma*. In some cases, the surprise factor compensates for the slightly lower level of control; in other cases, such as left *Ippon-seoi-nage*, the non-traditional attack is actually stronger.

TAILORED JACKETS

Tailored jackets are a common feature of contest judo. The advantages, according to their proponents, stem mainly from the difficulties they can cause opponents in getting and maintaining a secure sleeve grip. They simply do not give enough purchase for a strong and reliable grip.

But there are disadvantages too. Contest rules do legislate specifically on jacket limits, because judo is based on grips – without gripping, judo cannot exist. So, generally, although tailored jackets do cause gripping difficulties, they cannot be relied upon to prevent a grip being taken. Moreover, once an opponent has managed to get a grip, the wearer of the tailored jacket is at a distinct disadvantage, for he is trapped by that grip with no possibility of moving inside the jacket in order to get back on balance or evade a technique.

In addition, many current techniques are launched not from standard sleeve/collar grips, but from odd cross grips or from back of the jacket grips. Once again, the wearer of a tailored jacket can find himself at a disadvantage once a good grip has been attained – he can find himself in a prison of his own making with the area of his chest and shoulders easily controlled.

NEWAZA (GROUNDWORK)

The raised technical standard of players at national and international level now means that it is very difficult to do well consistently without a reasonable standard of groundwork. Weak groundwork is simply bad tactical preparation – not least because good groundwork is far easier to improve than throwing techniques. What's more, secure groundwork allows a player to attack with far more commitment in tachiwaza, because he is not worried that, should the attack fail, he will find himself on the ground.

There is another aspect to the relevance of strong newaza to modern contest judo. Most of the techniques recorded in this book will, at best, score ippon, but it is a fact of contest life that more often than not they will only result in a minor score. However, most offer outstanding opportunities for swift follow-ups into groundwork – but only if the player has the ability, and the confidence, to do so.

CHECKLIST ON MAIN OPPONENTS

An important part of the intelligent use of tactics is the preparation before a contest. How well do you know the opponents you are likely to meet? Do you know enough to make a basic plan of campaign, or are you going in completely uninformed, hoping that some divine spark will inspire you on the day? Here is a checklist worth noting:

1. Does your opponent have a right or left stance?
2. What grip does he need to launch his favourite attack pattern, and what are the possibilities for a counter throw?
3. Most good players usually have an attack to the other side. What is it? Does he change grips for it?
4. Does he attack from a static or moving position?
5. If he cannot get his favourite grips, what are his unorthodox moves? Leg grabs? Cross grips?
6. How well does he know you?
7. What are his countering skills like?
8. From what posture does he do his best work? Does he know your posture?
9. Does he attack on and around the red line? And does this indicate his newaza confidence – or lack of it?
10. What is feasible against his big throws – counter, avoidance or a block? If you are not sufficiently confident in any of them, you must attack first. All serious players should have a countering waza. If you just block, or avoid, you can lose on the number of attacks. If you can put in just one counter, you can inhibit an attacking pattern.

These are some pointers towards tactics. It is the prerogative of each player to ignore them, but it is the duty of each player to be aware of them for, as we have said, they are as much part of judo as a good fitness level or a good waza. It is salutary to consider that many of the throws illustrated in the photographs in this book would probably have been impossible without a sound knowledge of tactics.

5 The History of Judo

In 1936 Dr Jigoro Kano, the founder of Kodokan Judo, revealed his attitude towards the possible inclusion of judo in the Olympic Games in a conversation with Gunji Koizumi, the father of European judo, printed in the Budokwai Bulletin, April 1947:

'I have been asked by people of various sections as to the wisdom and possibility of judo being introduced with other games and sports at the Olympic Games. My view on the matter, at present, is rather passive. If it be the desire of other member countries, I have no objection. But I do not feel inclined to take any initiative. For one thing, judo in reality is not a mere sport or game. I regard it as a principle of life, art and science. In fact, it is a means for personal cultural attainment. Only one of the forms of judo training, so-called randori or free practice can be classed as a form of sport. Certainly, to some extent, the same may be said of boxing and fencing, but today they are practised and conducted as sports.

'Then the Olympic Games are so strongly flavoured with nationalism that it is possible to be influenced by it and to develop "Contest Judo", a retrograde form as ju-jitsu was before the Kodokan was founded.

'Judo should be free as art and science from any external influences, political, national, racial, financial or any other organised interest. And all things connected with it should be directed to its ultimate object, the "Benefit of Humanity". Human sacrifice is a matter of ancient history.

'Another point is the meaning of professionalism. With judo, we have no professionals in the same sense as other sports. No one is allowed to take part in public entertainment for personal gain. Teachers certainly receive remuneration for their services, but that is in no way degrading. The professional is held in high regard like the officers of a religious organisation or a professor in the educational world. Judo itself is held by us all in a position at the high altar. To reconcile this point of view with the Western idea is difficult. Success, or a satisfactory result of joining the Olympic Games would much depend on the degree of understanding of judo by the other participating countries.'

There could scarcely have been a clearer statement of the view held by Kano of judo as a sport in general, and contest judo in particular. Judged by this alone, a book with such a title should have no place in the international judo library, let alone even attempt to justify its claim that contest judo is the leading edge of judo technique.

But what is equally clear from even a brief perusal of judo history is that the role of contest throughout its eleven decades or so has been ambiguous to say the least. The first century has been studded with contest victories that, by themselves, have played a major role in the development of judo, both in Japan and outside. Arguably, without contest and its close links with the sports world, judo would not have survived into the modern world, and certainly not have developed into the force it is now.

On the other hand, it must be acknowledged that both Kano and Koizumi would probably be saddened in many ways to see the public face of judo in the closing years of the twentieth century with its emphasis on medals and on winning. From the founding of Kodokan Judo in 1882 and the opening of the first dojo in Eshoji Temple in Tokyo, Kano went to great pains to implement his ban on unorganised contests with rival members of older ju-jitsu schools. He wanted to disassociate judo from the reputation of petty thuggery that ju-jitsu commanded in the 1880s in Japan, and the difficult situation arose whereby strong fighters from the Kodokan were forced to endure taunts and insults in the street from rivals and even run away rather than fight back. The penalty for fighting was nothing less than dismissal from the Kodokan.

But that didn't stop more traditional challenges taking place. The tradition of Dojo Yaburi or dojo bashing was made respectable by custom. A challenger could visit a dojo, take on the top pupil and, if he beat him, challenge the teacher. If the challenger won, he could take the name-plate of the school from the door.

So, although Kano designated contest as just one aspect of training, along with kata, randori and mondo or discussion and question and answers, the early students of the Kodokan had to be able to fight. A number of unannounced visits to the Kodokan from ju-jitsu rivals took place in those early years, and, according to Kodokan records, the dojo never lost its name-plate. Certainly, it seemed that the combination of systematic training with the emphasis on the ju or yielding qualities of judo, managed to prevail over the more irregular training of most of the ju-jitsu schools of the time.

Kodokan history records one such event when, as usual, the rival ju-jitsu school chose a time when Kano was away. Shiro Saigo, one of the more bellicose of Kano's early pupils, could no longer stand the taunts of three muscled ju-jitsu exponents who had forced their way in and, against the advice of his companions, agreed to meet the challenge, despite the fact that he was little more than five foot. Four hip throws and a footsweep later, the challenger, one Matsugoro Okuda, retired with concussion. His two companions went the same way.

This immediately established the Kodokan as a school to be respected. It was followed by other victories. Hansuke Nakamura, the strongest member of the Ryoishin-toryu School and a teacher at the Police Headquarters, was flattened by Tsunejiro Tomita at a demonstration with *Tomoe-nage* and strangled with *Gyaku-juji-jime*. The master of the dojo intervened just before Nakamura went unconscious.

The greatest encounter took place at the Great Demonstration of the Martial Arts at the Police Headquarters in 1886. Although there were fifteen contests in all, the meeting between Entaro Kochi of the Tozuka School and Shiro Saigo of the Kodokan epitomised the principles of Kano's teaching, with his maximum efficiency from minimum effort. Saigo was dwarfed by his opponent, but although he was taken up into the air on numerous occasions and clearly put down hard now and again, his catlike ability to twist out of throws saved him from serious injury. Kochi became increasingly frustrated, impatient and tired. It was at this point that Saigo attacked with his famous *Yama-arashi*, or mountain storm, that floored Kochi so severely he was unable to get up to resume the contest.

The reputation of the Kodokan was further enhanced by the contest two years later between Sahujiro Yokoyama from the Kodokan over the hapless Nakamura. The detailed account of the fight gives an interesting insight into ju-jitsu encounters of the day.

The referee, director of the ju-jitsu section of Police Headquarters, ordered the fight to begin.

'For a while the two opponents, separated from each other by about four yards, stood still, looking into each other's eyes. Yokoyama was the first to move forward, while Nakamura, without changing his place, put himself into a position of left self-defence (*Hidari-jigotai*); the fighters got hold of each other's sleeves and slowly moved towards the left in order to attempt a preparatory action with the aim of destroying their respective positions of equilibrium. Five minutes, then ten passed without either of them risking an attack . . . For thirty minutes nothing happened, yet their foreheads were bathed in sweat.'

After forty minutes, Nakamura attempted a *Kata-guruma*. Yokoyama pushed him away and attempted an *Osoto-gari*. Nakamura was thrown and fell heavily, but was able to get up. A newaza sequence followed, with holds defended by *Shimewaza*. After the fight had been going for fifty minutes Nakamura managed to get a strong *Shiho-gatame*, but Yokoyama escaped.

After fifty-five minutes, with both of the opponents looking extremely tired, the referee ordered them to stop fighting. They ignored him. 'The honour of their respective schools was at stake and it was obvious that a draw would not satisfy either of them.'

The referee again attempted to separate them, but without success. 'They wanted a fight to a finish. Was the fight going to end in tragedy?' It took a plea from the Chief Commissioner himself to stop the fight, which was announced a draw.

The account of this fight indicates the contest conditions of the time. In many ways, rules maketh contests, and at this time there were virtually no rules, as is recounted in *Judo Shiai Shimpan Kitei*, a history of contest rules by Morishita and Murayama, translated by Syd Hoare.

'Originally, in ju-jitsu contests, there were no rules. If someone threw his opponent flat on his back, but the man just bounced up again, it didn't mean anything. The fight ended when one man gave up or was strangled or armlocked. Or died.'

The slow transition to a formal set of rules occurred because the whole objective of ju-jitsu, or judo as it became, changed.

However, some idea of the gradual introduction of rules can be seen by the system used by one ju-jitsu school, the Shinkiryu Rentai Ju-Jitsu, in 1895, where competitions were decided by a complex system of points, with fifteen points concluding the fight.

'Different techniques merited different points. A complete sutemi-waza or sacrifice throw was awarded ten points and what was considered an incompleted technique only nine points. Similarly, a complete koshi or hip technique merited eight points, whereas an incomplete technique was worth only seven. A hand technique, such as *Tai-otoshi*, was worth only six points.

'Katame-waza or groundwork techniques did not score highly – just two points for a full technique and one point for an incomplete technique.'

Behind these scores was the feeling that throws were highly regarded, yet were more difficult to achieve, while groundwork was relatively easy. In a real fight, throwing techniques were regarded as more effective because it was possible to deal with more than one assailant. On the other hand, while groundwork may be more efficacious, it was only possible to deal with one person at a time.

This indicates the convoluted attitude that existed in the ju-jitsu schools, including Kodokan Judo, in the last years of the nineteenth century in regard to contest. Initially, contest was equated with fighting or duels, the archetypal struggle of one man against another. In short, war. On the other hand, it was a useful medium for testing skills, both in terms of the relative merits of one school's skill against another and also in terms of the personal attainment of individuals.

It was this question of personal attainment that was the prime interest of Kano, who was first and foremost an educator. Although he

Jigoro Kano, the founder of judo.

Gungi Koizumi – father of European judo.

Olympic and World Champion Yashuiro Yamashita (Japan) with 1964 Olympic gold medallist Anton Geesink (Holland).

could see the need to prove the worth of Kodokan Judo against other ju-jitsu schools, he was equally eager to concentrate on contest as an educational medium as soon as it was possible. The gradual evolution of contest rules from the very early days to the complex list that exists now reflects the change in attitude towards contest, away from the platform of judo as a martial art, away from judo as personal education, and towards judo as a sport. Kano, Koizumi and others, such as T. P. Leggett, for many years the senior Western exponent of judo, could see the direction judo was taking and, in many ways, regretted it despite its undeniable advantages in the popularisation of judo. But Leggett himself recalls vividly how much rougher judo was in the Japanese dojos before the Second World War than afterwards, when it became more closely aligned with the sports movement. This development came as one of the results of the evolution of contest rules.

In 1899 a set of thirteen rules were formulated by the Dai Nippon Butokukai, or Great Japan Martial Virtues Association. This brought together many of the ju-jitsu masters under the chairmanship, so-to-speak, of Jigoro Kano, which indicates the status of the relatively youthful Kodokan Judo. These rules included the following:

1. Contests were run on the basis of throwing and groundwork techniques.
2. A fight was won by two ippons.
3. After an appropriate time, hiki-wake or draw could be called by the referee.
4. Ippon and waza-ari scores were counted.
5. In joint locks, it was forbidden to attack the toes, fingers, wrists or ankles.

At this time, Kodokan Judo had not been established throughout Japan, although it was growing rapidly. The following year, 1900, Kodokan Judo formed its own set of rules based on the Butokukai, but with two main changes.:

1. Under 1st Dan, no kansetsu-waza or locks, were allowed.
2. The proportion of groundwork to standing had to be about 60–40 per cent. This was introduced to prevent specialist groundwork ju-jitsu schools coming out into a contest with the simple aim of dragging their opponent down in any fashion and polishing him off on the ground.

In 1916 another set of rule changes was made by the Kodokan, mainly in an attempt to reduce the serious injuries that still occurred in contests. The main change concerned two techniques, *Ashi-garami* and *Dojime*.

Ashi-garami (the last technique in *Katame-no-kata*) and *Dojime* (kidney squeeze), were banned. It was felt that although *Ashi-garami* was difficult to use against an opponent of equal ability, it was extremely dangerous against a lesser opponent. And the *Dojime*, when effectively applied, tended to damage the internal organs.

In 1925 there was yet another series of changes. Once again the emphasis was on safety and on promoting the throwing aspects of judo, which were being threatened by the predominance of groundwork. For the first time it appeared in the rules that judo contests had to begin with tachiwaza. Until this point, it seems, it was theoretically possible for one contestant to start the contest lying on his back. The groundwork strength of one particular ju-jitsu school, the Kosen Judo School, had promoted these changes.

The new rules established in 1925 included:

1. Judo started with opponents standing up.
2. There were a series of restrictions on the manner in which an opponent could be taken to the ground.
3. Knee locks and spine locks were forbidden.
4. No joints were to be locked apart from the elbow.
5. It was forbidden to scissor the neck between the legs.

6. It was forbidden to put the fingers into the opening of the jacket or trousers.

It is interesting to speculate that without these rules, judo would not have been a throwing sport. It is extremely difficult to throw someone who is just concerned with dragging his opponent to the ground in any manner possible. And with contests becoming increasingly regarded as the pinnacle of judo training, there seemed little point in practising techniques that would not be allowed in competition. In this way, the development of the contest rules played an extremely influential role in the shaping of judo.

Even during the 1940s, there were major rule changes. In 1941, for instance, penalties were introduced for going outside the fighting area, as well as further restrictions for going from standing to groundwork. Also, the function of referees was more clearly defined.

More detailed rules were also made which, indirectly, give a vivid picture of what judo was like at the time. They also speak volumes about the ingenuity of judo men to avoid what they don't like:

1. To avoid groundwork, it was not allowed to put the feet in the belt or inside the judogi.
2. It was forbidden to break strangles by pulling on the fingers.
3. It was forbidden to put the hands or feet on the face.
4. It was forbidden to bind the opponent's hand with the bottom of the jacket or the belt.
5. In order to go to the ground, one could not grab hold of one or two legs.
6. It was forbidden, in order to go for a draw, to grab hold of one lapel and one sleeve on the same side for any length of time.
7. Any actions that aim at the draw were forbidden.
8. Any actions that take the opponent into groundwork from the start were forbidden.

Jigoro Kano died in 1938, by which time the modern contest structure within judo was already established. The All-Japan Championships were an annual event and were regarded very much as the high point of the judo year. Moreover, despite the lack of weight categories, they were not entirely dominated by heavyweights.

In Europe, too, there were contests on a fairly regular basis, although international events between two countries, such as Great Britain and Germany, were exclusively team competitions. With the development of European judo being directed by the pure integrity of Gunji Koizumi, who was primarily motivated by the ethical and educational principles enshrined in judo as he saw it, individual championships remained something of an anathema.

However, here again there existed an ambiguity. One of the reasons why Britain took such a commanding lead in the development of judo outside Japan was partly because of the industry of Koizumi; but also partly because British judo, and in particular English judo, was well regarded – due, in large part, to the fierce but effective training of Yukio Tani.

If Koizumi provided the theoretical framework for judo, it was Tani who, in the early days before his stroke in 1935, provided the practical experience. For Tani, who arrived in England in 1899, established himself by taking on all comers in the music-halls and, reputedly, losing only once – to another younger and fitter Japanese judoka.

Tani, therefore, scarcely embodied the finest principles of judo as envisaged by Kano and Koizumi; but on the other hand his technical ability could not be denied. It was this contest strength that fed its way into the veins of British judo, into such leading exponents as T. P. Leggett, and then, by direct transmission, to the succeeding generation that proved eminently successful at the European and World Championships when they came.

But that was years in the future. The early

appeal of judo in Europe generally and Britain in particular was that it offered a form of self-defence where, theoretically at least, the small, trained and intelligent man could overcome ugly brawn. This was palpably demonstrated by Yukio Tani in the music-halls and went on to be the theme of judo for decades in an era of no weight categories. Even after the Second World War, and to some extent still today, the public view of judo is that it enables the exponent to deal with most likely opponents short of Super-man or the possessor of a machine gun.

Those who studied and practised judo came to know fairly swiftly that it was true that a small but skilled judo man or woman could deal remarkably well with an opponent twice their size, and that remains true today; but only while there was an equally great differential in their level of skills. This patently obvious fact was denied or overlooked or punctured by blasts of theory for decades – in the West at least. The reason was partly because it represented a pure ideal, and ideals were a very important element of the early appeal of judo.

When judo arrived in the West, it appealed as a combat form to the educated man and woman. Many people who tried out judo or ju-jitsu in the 1920s would not have been so readily prepared to train in a boxing gym. The fact that judo came tinged with Eastern mysticism packaged it nicely for a generation that was just discovering the practice of Buddhism and other Eastern philosophies.

Judo as a medium for personal development was unstintingly promoted by Koizumi from the day he opened The Budokwai in London in 1918. It permeated his teaching and, from the first issues of The Budokwai Bulletin in April 1945, it was a constant theme in his articles. Again and again, Koizumi or correspondents hammered home the dangers of allowing 'competitions and contests to become the means and end of life's interest'. Koizumi argued that judo would suffer were it reduced to so-called 'Contest Judo' which would transform an 'ideal into dogmatic –ism, thus producing egocentric –ists and –ians'.

This atmosphere, of regarding the practice of judo as something closer to a religion than a sport, must be remembered in order to appreciate the dilemma that British judo faced when the whole paraphernalia of sport contest – or, as Koizumi, once described it, contestics – began to emerge in the post-war period.

Not just for years, but for decades, the British judo establishment, one of the foremost outside Japan, maintained a rearguard action amidst anxious public and private debates over the appropriateness and usefulness of competition in judo. After all, had Jigoro Kano not decreed that contest was only one small part of judo? Had he not said: 'I did not attach exclusive importance to contest training, but aimed at a combination of contest exercising and the training of mind and body'? And was there not a very real danger of individuals suffering delusions of personal grandeur by becoming a 'Champion'? And where would it end? Would judo become like boxing or wrestling, with showmanship, bulging biceps, publicity overkill and high stakes?

As is often the case, the disciples were more severe than the master. Kano himself was Japan's representative on the International Olympic Committee and was thus closely involved with the development of the international sports movement. Despite his statement to Koizumi in 1936, there are many indications that he had a flexible view of contest and sport. A few years earlier, he said: 'I can see that competition can be useful for the promotion of judo, and in the future, it may be necessary to have a world championships.' What's more, he certainly condoned if not actively promoted the creation of a national championship in Japan. Each year, from 1930, the best contest men of judo from both the Kodokan and the Butokukai (there was a great amount of rivalry between the two) competed in front of the Emperor.

Despite this clear lead from Japan, contests in Europe before the Second World War were restricted to team events, at international, national and club level, and grading contests. Even when the All-Japan Championships resumed in 1948, Europe and especially Britain refused to follow in its footsteps, although by then there were not only enough practitioners to make it a practical proposition, but there was even the machinery to deal with it.

The size of the judo movement was expanding beyond the easy control of one club; in Britain, for convenience, clubs around the country affiliated to the British fountain-head of judo, The Budokwai. In 1948, under the inspiration of Gunji Koizumi, the British Judo Association was founded, followed rapidly by the European Judo Union. One of the main stated objects of the EJU was 'to establish international conditions and rules for contests'.

Even at this point, the rules under which contest took place were quite varied: sometimes the best of three ippons, or one ippon, or waza-ari and ippon. As the pressures for regular international competitions increased, the debate for the defence of judo in its pure form continued. In 1950, Koizumi wrote in the Budokwai Bulletin: 'Matches or contests are a part of training in judo, not an end nor a means of glorifying individual or collective superiority as is the case for most sports. This uniqueness of judo must be retained to save judo from being degraded to a mere competitive sport . . . striving for an ideal is life and judo. Attaining is not in the prospectus for mortal man.'

It is difficult not to admire the integrity of Gunji Koizumi who must have felt a little like King Canute as the debate hotted up. But he was not alone. The following year, the Bulletin carried a letter from a Mr Wal Blau who noted that on the Continent judo was changing all too quickly and pleaded that judo should not be allowed to 'get caught in the Olympic vortex' for it would encourage 'a type of ruthlessness both inimical to the spirit of judo and sour to our taste'. He continues: 'The public, led by a sceptical press, would load on the shoulders of the British team the full weight of British Honour, and the fate of English Sport would be made to hang on a *Harai Goshi*.

'I make a plea that we shall not Westernise this gentle art we have adopted. There are European sports aplenty. Boxing, wrestling and the like; each attracts its own crowd and the more the blood the bigger the gate since in its essence these spectacles are little more than exhibitions of muscular strength and ability to absorb punishment.

'Judo, the little Eastern flower, blooms quietly, away from the silly plaudits of a gaping crowd whose ignorance would dismiss it as a fake or decry it as lot of dirty tripping.'

Alack and alas, this heartfelt expression fell on deaf ears for the most part, although it is difficult not to sympathise in some ways, and even acknowledge that, to some extent, he was right. The onset of contest judo was to change the face of judo as he knew it – in fact, that very year.

On 5 and 6 December, in the Palais des Sports, Paris, the first European Judo Championships took place in front of an enthusiastic audience of 15,000 people, led by none other than Mr Risei Kano, second son of the founder and President of the Kodokan. The rules followed were Kodokan Contest Rules with waza-ari scored, and one ippon ending the contest. There were five men in each team, but no weight categories.

France beat Holland easily 4–1. England met an inexperienced Italian team and won 4–1. France then demolished Belgium 4–1. England then drew against West Germany, with one draw, two wins and two losses. The captains fought off, with Geoffrey Gleeson deciding the match with a waza-ari from an *Osoto-gari*. In the final France beat England decisively with four wins and one draw.

On the second day, the individual grade

championships were held. The categories were Brown Belt and under, 1st Dan, 2nd Dan, 3rd Dan, and Open. One of the most exciting matches was in the 3rd Dan event, when Britain's Gleeson faced Jean de Herdt, the winner of the French Championships. After five minutes, there was no score, and a three-minute extension was given. After those three minutes, there was again no score, and a further five-minute extension was given. It was in this last quarter that the Frenchman managed to counter Gleeson for a waza-ari. They met again in the final of the Open with the same result. Immediately following the event, Jean de Herdt was promoted to 4th Dan by Mr Kano.

The undoubted success of the first European Championships, both from the point of view of judo and as a public spectacle, ensured its continuity. The question now was not whether international events should be organised on a regular basis, but whether weight categories should be introduced. This was an equally heated debate. Koizumi argued against their introduction. 'Judo is a principle and, as an element in nature, it has many facets of manifestation', he wrote in the Budokwai Bulletin. Percy Sekine, a Budokwai Black Belt argued the opposite. If weight categories were not introduced, contest judo at international level would become the preserve of huge judoka, he declared, and added that the Olympic ideal would only be truly served by weight categories.

Defenders of the faith could point to the report by Charles Palmer, then studying in Japan, of the All-Japan Championships of that year. One of the most spectacular performers was Osawa who, at 145lb, beat Endo (182lb) in an extraordinary manner – which also indicated the danger of contesting on the customary raised dais of the time. 'Osawa beat Endo with an extremely fast left-hand *Tai-otoshi* after throwing him completely out of the mat area and into the crowd with the best *Osoto-gari* I have ever seen. Endo must have levelled off at about seven feet from the floor (nearly five feet off the mat). Consequently, he was rather dazed and required a few minutes' rest before he could continue.' However, Osawa was beaten by a bigger – and equally skilful – opponent, Yoshimatsu, in the following round.

The issues of weight categories, of international contests, as well as other topics such as refereeing, rules, and gradings, made the creation of the International Judo Federation a necessity, and it met first in 1951. In 1952 the IJF and the EJU met in Venice and, in a series of marathon meetings, worked to hammer out some of the problems. Mr Risei Kano was offered the presidency of the IJU. East Germany was given observer status to the EJU.

Britain proposed that annual European Championships should be abolished, or at least held every two or three years. The reasons given were partly organisational, but also because there was 'a tendency to lose the spirit of judo in Championship conditions'. France objected, and was given the right to run the 1952 Championships, with a kyu-grade competition; individual Dan grade competitions (1st, 2nd and 3rd Dan events); Open; and a team competition with five men.

In the ensuing discussion on weight categories, Britain, France, Belgium and Holland were against their introduction. France suggested that individual countries might care to try out weight category events on a domestic basis only. Three weight categories were suggested: 68 kilos and below; 80 kilos and below; over 80 kilos.

The ground was gradually being prepared for judo in the modern world. Having declined to stage the 1952 European Championships, Britain agreed to host the 1953 event. This was especially notable in that it confirmed the outstanding talent of one man in particular, the six foot six inch Dutchman Anton Geesink, who had won the Open the year before at the age of 18, and repeated his success, as well as leading his country to victory in the team event.

The success of the European Championships and the appointment of Risei Kano to the presidency of the IJF meant that it was only a matter of time before Jigoro Kano's prophesy was fulfilled, and the first World Championships were held. They were held in Tokyo on 3 May 1956, with 21 nations taking part. The results, with Japan's Natsui and Yoshimatsu coming first and second, and Geesink and France's Courtine third and fourth, were not carried in the Budokwai Bulletin. Instead, there was a slightly sad report from Mr Koizumi, who noted that Britain still did not have its own national event.

Nevertheless, Britain's contest strength was shown in the European team event in 1957 with a convincing win, the first in what was to prove a run of three straight victories. It is against this backdrop that a reluctance to participate in the individual events must be seen.

Most of the contests that took place by this time were conducted under Kodokan rules, although the formal Kodokan time of contests – with preliminaries sometimes lasting 15 minutes and finals 20 minutes – were not observed. But the use of three judges, and of yusei-gachi (often awarded with the reason appended) had already been introduced. In 1958 there were further rule changes which affected contests dramatically.

1. Stepping out of the area became a prohibited act.
2. One warning was reckoned as an adverse cause for awarding yusei-gachi.
3. Two warnings were equal to near waza-ari.
4. Three warnings, waza-ari, but it was not reckoned to form ippon with another waza-ari.
5. Four warnings, meant loss of contest.

The same year, the second World Championships took place, again in Tokyo, with 10-minute preliminary contests and a 20-minute final. Japan once more dominated, with Sone, Kaminaga and Yamashiki winning the first three places, and France's Pariset coming fourth. Geesink was thrown for ippon with a footsweep by Yamashiki.

Although Japan and other countries still held out against the introduction of weight categories at World Championship level, they were seen for the first time in a major international event in the 1959 European Championships in Holland, and unfortunately coincided with a disastrous affair in many ways.

It was certainly a complicated event. There were the team championships, with no weight categories which were won for the third time in a row by Britain, fielding a five-man team led by Charles Palmer, 4th Dan. Then there were the grade championships, with five categories, from 1st Dan to 4th Dan and Open, the latter won by Geesink again. Then, for the first time, there were the weight category contests, which were, according to contemporary reports, technically excellent, although they were not taken very seriously by some countries: neither Britain nor France entered competitors, leaving the field open for Holland, with Geesink again winning in the heavyweights.

But there were organisational problems. The mats were described as 'disgraceful', being 'soft and soggy and covered with a slack canvas'. Apparently, the canvas was so slack that one competitor managed to take hold of great handfuls to stabilise himself in newaza.

The refereeing was very questionable in some cases, with many of the referees being 'low grades and overawed by the occasion and the competitors'.

There was also an ugly crowd scene. A small Dutch patriot walked across the arena waving a small paper Netherlands flag, which was snatched from him by a burly Austrian who proceeded to tear it up. This was seen by Geesink, waiting patiently on the mat for the start of the heavyweight finals. He started to approach the Austrian, but was restrained by the Dutch team manager. However, by this time, the Austrian had taken to his heels in shock at the thought of a confrontation with the mighty Geesink, and, unfortunately, ran straight into a large crowd of Dutch fans. A fight broke out and the Austrian was unceremoniously dumped over the end of the stands. Once calm had been restored the heavyweight final started, but was all over in less than thirty seconds when Geesink threw Sinek of West Germany with *Uchimata*.

By the end of these Championships, it was clear that judo was about to move in to another era. The increasing importance of the results in the European Championships, and the likelihood that Japanese domination at world events would be broken, meant that contests were taking on a different character.

'It was common to see overweight men doing judo, although with skill and speed,' recalls Mr Palmer, who played such a crucial role in the British team during its three winning years. No one was much concerned with gripping skills – players just took what they could get and made it serve their purpose. 'The object of everyone was to achieve the perfect throw – that is, a throw which was made without any effort.'

In the middle 1950s there were more counter throws, because fighters, concerned with the principle of good posture, would stand upright. As the new decade dawned, *Jigotai*, and even deep *Jigotai*, was becoming increasingly common – some reports indicate competitors coming out to face an opponent with one hand trailing on the ground. This affected technique, of course, and was largely responsible for *Hane-goshi*, once one of the highest scoring techniques, virtually disappearing from the international contest mat.

Referees found themselves increasingly unable to cope with the pressures placed on them by the events and the competitors – after all, there were no international refereeing courses.

Nevertheless, judo was poised for a major breakthrough, and four events occurred, one

after another, that were finally to establish judo as an international sport, to the delight of many and the genuine regret of quite a few.

In 1961, in the third World Championships, held in Paris (the first time outside Japan), Anton Geesink at last broke the stranglehold maintained by the Japanese on judo by beating Sone with an unorthodox hold in the final, after 8 minutes and 20 seconds. That hold was later classified as *Mune-gatame*. This was regarded as a breakthrough for Western judo, although it was acknowledged that Geesink was an exception: not only was he the largest competitor, but also appeared to be the fittest and strongest; he did not carry any fat at all; and, most importantly, he possessed both good throwing and groundwork skills.

Geesink's win forced everyone to look forward three years to the Tokyo Olympics when judo was to be included on the premier sports calendar for the first time. The great question was whether the Japanese would be able to find the answer to the Dutchman's strength.

The following year, in the European Championships in Essen, West Germany, there was another major development: the first appearance on the international judo scene of a team from the Soviet Union. This proved as shocking to the established Western judo countries as Sone's loss must have been to the Japanese. The Soviet team was fundamentally a group of sambo wrestlers wearing judo jackets and trying to keep to the judo rules. In sambo wrestling the competitor must throw the opponent directly on to his back yet remain standing for an outright win. Otherwise, it is necessary to follow up on the ground. Holds and armlocks are allowed, but no strangles.

The sambo/judo team burst upon the 1962 European Championships, surprising most of their opponents with their fitness, their fierce resolve to win at, it seemed, any costs, and their totally unorthodox techniques. They declined to grip normally, stood at odd angles, and grabbed at the legs. The judo traditionalists didn't quite know what to make of it – and the English team were flummoxed. Charles Palmer, there for the first time as a referee, remembers that 'the only fears I had for the British team were those of personal injury rather than defeat'. The British team lost to the Soviets, who were, however, beaten by Holland. Nevertheless, individual members went on to win five medals in the other events – no mean feat in their first international judo competition.

If this was the first event to display the huge potential of the Soviet Union – which was clearly prompted by the imminent inclusion of judo into the Olympics – it was also the last to feature the individual grade competitions. This was largely due to the Soviet Union, whose players appeared on the contest mats wearing belts of all colours and were clearly quite happy to undermine Japanese tradition by changing the belts from blue to black with impunity. From the 1963 European Championships, the individual events were to be based solely on weight categories.

Japan, too, was looking ahead and, in November 1962, held the first championships which involved weight categories.

Thus the scene was set for the Olympics themselves. Each country could send two competitors in each of the three weight categories and the Open. Britain, which still did not have a national championships of its own had, at the same time, to contend with as many as fourteen other judo organisations in addition to the BJA. National Olympic Trials were held with representatives from the British Judo Council and Amateur Judo Association invited. In the event, the exercise was an academic one, for none of the BJC or AJA competitors got through to the final rounds.

The Olympic Judo Competition in 1964 was held in the new Budokan Hall in Tokyo. All the categories were fought on the basis of pools and knockout rounds. Curiously, in addition to the referee and two corner judges, there was a special panel of judges overlooking the contest area and they had the right to

intervene with their own decision. This occurred in the final of the lightweight competition won by Japan's Nakatani over Haenni (Switzerland). The middleweight was won, as expected, by Okano, and the heavyweight by Inokuma, making three gold medals for Japan. But, also as expected, Japan's Kaminaga was unable to withstand the power and technique of Anton Geesink, who was well ahead throughout the final, eventually catching Kaminaga on the ground and holding him down with *Kesa-gatame* for ippon.

Thus, judo established itself for the first time before an Olympic audience. The internationalisation of judo continued with the election to the presidency of the IJF of Britain's Charles Palmer in 1965, an event which certainly affected the development of contest judo over the next fifteen years, and in a way marked a very definite chapter in its growth.

Palmer, along with the rest of the judo fraternity, presumed that with the appearance of judo in the 1964 Olympics, its future as a regular feature on the programme was assured. But this proved not to be the case, as he discovered as late as 1966.

At this point, he began the serious campaign for its inclusion on the full programme. He almost succeeded in making it a late entry in the 1968 event, but eventually had to be content with the acceptance on the 1972 programme in Munich. If the IOC presidency had remained in Japanese hands, it is doubtful whether judo would have emerged from the political lobbying to take its rightful place on the Olympic programme.

Changes continued during this time, however. In 1966 the weight categories were subdivided into five weights – U63k, U70k, U80k, U93k, Over 93k – and the Open, in time for the 1967 World Championships in Salt Lake City.

The mid-1960s also saw changes in Britain's domestic events. The death of Koizumi on 15 April 1965 was very clearly the end of an era, for although he had taken a back seat

Two outstanding heavyweights, Angelo Parisi (left) and Wilhelm Ruska.

Neil Adams, 1981 World Champion and five times European Champion.

Charles Palmer, for many years President of the IJF.

from the international and even national scene, his presence was still very much felt.

Perhaps not coincidentally, 1965 also saw the first British Open Championships, held in Crystal Palace, well behind other European countries.

The next main international change concerned scoring in judo. Though Palmer is generally regarded as the main instigator of koka and yuko in judo, he has stated that his personal standpoint was very different: 'I was in favour of waza-ari and ippon only, and where neither contestant managed to score, both were eliminated.'

But both he and the IJF committee did acknowledge that changes were necessary. Too often, a late attack by a contestant claimed the attention of the referee and won a decision, although that contestant may have made only one attack in the whole contest.

'Our primary concern was to devise a system where the right man would win – which was not always the case with waza-ari and ippon,' remembers Palmer. Yuko was already being used in Japan, and a kind of koka was declared but not placed on the score-board – kinsa, or win by 'a very small amount'. Palmer and his IJF committee produced the idea of koka, and, despite Japanese opposition, it was rapidly accepted throughout the world.

Many traditionalists, however, saw this as a retrograde step, arguing that it would see the advent of 'koka' judo, but it was regarded then, and generally now, as fairer both to referees and players. Even in the early World Championships and Olympics, referees had been attempting to keep a score in their heads for the minor attacks, and it was far easier to place those on the board. So, by the 1976 Olympics, not only were the koka and yuko part of modern judo, but so were the red mats denoting the edge of the fighting area.

Following the 1977 World Championships in Vienna the weight categories were further subdivided, at the instigation of the Soviet Union which was always looking for opportunities for more medals. The system now in use was established, with seven weight categories: U60k, U65k, U71k, U78k, U86k, U95k, O95k – though the Open weight category was retained.

Just how much judo was now in the modern sports arena, with all the political implications, could be seen by the disastrous affair of the 1979 World Championships due to be held in Spain. The Spanish government had agreed to issue visas to all members of the IJF, but, two weeks from the start of the event, it was continuing to withhold visas from the Taiwan contingent. The Taiwanese had, that year, already experienced difficulty in attending other world championships which had gone ahead despite host governments refusing to issue visas.

But Palmer and the IOC committee refused to be browbeaten by the Spanish government and summarily cancelled the event – though not before strenuous efforts were made to host the Championships elsewhere despite the short notice. It is significant that judo has never since been involved in such political threats – it was a precedent that other sports could do well to follow.

No mention has been made so far of women's judo. It has taken much longer for a competition structure for women to evolve, not least because of the original attitude of Kano to women's involvement in judo. Though records exist that he gave private judo lessons to women quite early on in the days of Kodokan Judo, it was not until 1923 that an experimental class for women was started at the Kodokan – and then the main emphasis was on Juno-Kata and technique training.

By that time women had been accepted as members of The Budokwai, and they were to be a continuous feature of judo in the West as the years unfolded. Nevertheless, they faced a certain amount of prejudice – for some years they were restricted to their ladies' class at The Budokwai, and only exceptionally strong judokas such as Christine Child, eventual

European Champion, were allowed to do randori with the men in the main dojo.

Women did take part in grading contests, but it was not until the late 1950s and early 1960s that competitions for women began to become fairly commonplace.

Other countries were still far behind Britain at this point. Rusty Kanokogi, the most capable American female judoka of the time, cut her hair short, taped her breasts flat, and entered the team event in the 1958 New York State YMCA Championships – and won it. However, the medal was taken away from her and 'male' discreetly entered into the title of all future championships to prevent a recurrence.

But it was becoming evident that the contest side of women's judo could no longer be ignored. In 1966, in Liverpool, the first Team Championships for Women were held – though under some extraordinary con-

ditions. The event took place behind closed doors; and in addition to the normal scores, the women were marked on points of skill, style, quality of movement and spirit – and these marks could and did affect the results. One wonders how the men would have fared under such controls.

The success of the event, however, resulted in further team championships. In 1969, the event was transferred to Crystal Palace – though the curtains were delicately drawn to shield the event from the casual viewer. In 1971, the first British Open for Women marked the arrival of the international competitive event.

This was followed, over the next four years, by a remarkable growth of events all over Europe. In 1974, in Italy, a trial European Championships was organised, followed in 1975 by the first official European Championships for Women in West Germany. By

Brigitte Deydier, three times World Champion.

Ingrid Berghmans, World Champion.

the late 1970s women were pressing the IJF for permission to hold the first World Championships, and these finally took place in New York in 1980.

For the next three world events, the women alternated the years with the men. There was little doubt that, despite the scepticism of many top ranking men in the judo world, the effect of the world and European contests was to lift the standard of women's judo not just at the top competitive level, but at grass roots too.

Japan suffered badly in these relatively early contest days for women, for it was not until 1978 that the home of judo held its first competition for women. But gradually, especially through the promotion of the Japanese Invitation Championships for Women – The Fukuoka Cup – the women of Japan began to make more of an international impact.

Characteristically, the Soviet Union did not show any interest until it became evident that women's judo was going to be included in the Olympics. In fact, the fight for Olympic inclusion and parity with men was not an easy one. It was only after a series of set-backs that the Olympic Committee finally agreed to women's judo being accepted as a demonstration sport in Seoul in 1988, and full inclusion in Barcelona in 1992.

But the modern pattern for contest judo was set on British soil in 1986 when, at the Commonwealth Games, men's judo was seen side by side with women's judo. Though it was formally classed as a demonstration event, it proved to be one of the most exciting spectacles of the Games. It was followed by a similar arrangement for the 1987 European Championships in Paris, and the 1987 World Championships in Essen. This brings judo in line with the general sports trend where women compete in the same arena as men.

The evolution of contest judo has been long and convoluted. Many of the intervening steps seem either quaint or unnecessary and even downright objectionable now, but they have to be seen in the context of the prevailing ideas and conditions.

In some respects, it could be argued that the caution and reluctance expressed by Kano and Koizumi towards contest judo was well-founded. Winning has become all-important. The prophesy of both that contest judo would be regarded by many as the pinnacle of judo and that as a result the finer ideals of judo would be lost has, perhaps, proved true.

Few people are as well placed to comment on the changing face of judo as Charles Palmer, who, as President of the IJF for many years, oversaw some of the major changes. He comments that, on a technical level, contest judo has become more exciting, though, paradoxically, there are fewer spectacular throwing techniques. There is no doubt, however, that the technical level of ground-work has improved dramatically.

He feels that, as Kano predicted, contest judo has aided the popularisation of judo enormously, and that the physical standards of the contest men and women have risen as a result. But he declares that a lot of self-discipline among those involved in judo has been lost, along with a strong sense of sportsmanship.

'I still believe that judo is not just a physical activity, that the balance between the mind and the body is vital, and that expressions which sound a little trite now, such as "working together for mutual welfare and benefit" still should have meaning.'

The future remains a question mark. Having apparently finally sorted out the weight categories, the place of women in judo, the main problems of contest rules, and having established an international standard for referees, it could have been presumed that contest judo could look forward to a period of consolidation rather than change.

But that is not so. The final chapter in the transformation of judo from its martial art origins into judo as an Olympic sport capable of being played by children in schools was perhaps written in the programme of the

Olympic Games in Seoul in 1988. For the first time, the Open category, the premier event in judo, has been wiped from the calendar.

No more, under the Olympic flag at least, will a man weighing little more than 80 kilos, face the huge men of judo, testing his speed, skill, daring and fitness against bulk. Even in the fifteen years or so since the Olympic judo era began, contest judo has seen some stunning upsets in the Open category, when smaller men have managed to overcome the heavyweights.

The most consistent success by a non-heavyweight in recent years has been achieved by the Belgian light-heavyweight Robert van de Walle, who won bronzes in the Open event in the World Championships in 1981 and 1983. And in an extraordinary performance in the European Championships in 1986, Robert Seisenbacher followed up his win in the middleweight (U86k) category by winning a silver in the Open.

However, the record books show that such feats are becoming increasingly rare, as heavyweights improve both in fitness and technical ability. In a way, the Open category was simply becoming another heavyweight event, and the harsh practical eye of Olympic organisation, worried about the growing numbers in all sports, ordered its abolition. At a stroke, therefore, it cut what forlorn links remained with the martial arts tradition, a tradition which dictates that formal contest is, at the very least, a preparation for the life and death duel, not a symbolic substitute for it.

And there are more changes to come, changes that will make the traditionalists hang their heads even lower in shame. For the judo world is being asked to accept further alterations and compromises in the hope that it will increase the popularity of the sport.

If judo is going to attract wider media attention, and thus attract wider audiences, the television pundits argue, it should improve its presentation. Competitors could wear different coloured judogi, one perhaps blue and the other white. This is scheduled to be introduced in the 1988 European Championships. Wider popularisation also demands that there is a need to simplify the scoring system – perhaps by adopting a method of accumulating points as in wrestling. And, to further serve the whims of the media, judo contests may follow the pattern of preliminaries on one day and finals on another, a pattern experimented with at the 1987 European Championships in Paris.

At the time of writing, final decisions on these changes have yet to be taken.

Clearly, there are years of further change ahead.

Appendix: Competition Results

MEN'S EUROPEAN CHAMPIONSHIPS

1969 Ostend, Belgium

Category	Name	Country
Lightweight	Feist	France
Light-middleweight	Rudman	USSR
Middleweight	Bondarenko	USSR
Light-heavyweight	Snyders	Holland
Heavyweight	Ruska	Holland
Open	Ruska	Holland

1970 Berlin, East Germany

Category	Name	Country
Lightweight	Mounier	France
Light-middleweight	Hendel	East Germany
Middleweight	Jacks	Great Britain
Light-heavyweight	Pokatajew	USSR
Heavyweight	Glahn	West Germany
Open	Hennig	East Germany

1971 Gothenburg, Sweden

Category	Name	Country
Lightweight	Mounier	France
Light-middleweight	Hendel	East Germany
Middleweight	Auffray	France
Light-heavyweight	Howiller	East Germany
Heavyweight	Ruska	Holland
Open	Kusnetsor	USSR

1972 The Hague, Holland

Category	Name	Country
Lightweight	Mounier	France
Light-middleweight	Hotger	East Germany
Middleweight	Coche	France
Light-heavyweight	Parisi	Great Britain
Heavyweight	Ruska	Holland
Open	Ruska	Holland

1973 Madrid, Spain

Category	Name	Country
Lightweight	Melnichenko	USSR
Light-middleweight	Hotger	East Germany
Middleweight	Jacks	Great Britain
Light-heavyweight	Rouge	France
Heavyweight	Ojeda	Spain
Open	Novikov	USSR

1974 London, Great Britain

Category		Name	Country
Lightweight	1	Melnichenko	USSR
	2	Da Costa	Great Britain
	3	Algisi	France
	3	Pitskhelauri	USSR
Light-middleweight	1	Kruger	East Germany
	2	Dvoinikov	USSR
	3	Gautier	France
	3	Dorbant	West Germany
Middleweight	1	Coche	France
	2	Reiter	Poland
	3	Debelius	Great Britain
	3	Adamczyk	Poland
Light-heavyweight	1	Zuvela	Yugoslavia
	2	Neureuther	West Germany
	3	Starbrook	Great Britain
	3	Lorenz	East Germany
Heavyweight	1	Onashvilli	USSR
	2	Dolman	Holland
	3	Zuckschwerdt	East Germany
	3	Berthet	France
Open	1	Novikov	USSR
	2	Chochosvilli	USSR
	3	Varga	Hungary
	3	Zuckschwerdt	East Germany

1975 Lyons, France

Category		Name	Country
Lightweight	1	Reissmann	East Germany
	2	Pitskhelauri	USSR
	3	Waksnin	Poland
	3	Delvingt	France
Light-middleweight	1	Nvezerov	USSR
	2	Dvoinikov	USSR
	3	Hotger	East Germany
	3	Kruger	East Germany
Middleweight	1	Reiter	Poland
	2	Barkaliev	USSR
	3	Adamczyk	Poland
	3	Volosov	USSR
Light-heavyweight	1	Lorenz	East Germany
	2	Rouge	France
	3	Starbrook	Great Britain
	3	Kharchiladze	USSR
Heavyweight	1	Nidzeradze	USSR
	2	Novikov	USSR
	3	Novak	Czechoslovakia
	3	Zuckschwerdt	East Germany
Open	1	Onashvilli	USSR
	2	Chochosvilli	USSR
	3	Zuckschwerdt	East Germany
	3	Adelaar	East Germany

1976 Kiev, USSR

Category		Name	Country
Lightweight	1	Tountchik	Hungary
	2	Zourabiani	USSR
	3	Aljisi	France
	3	Delvingt	France
Light-middleweight	1	Dvoinikov	USSR
	2	Hotger	East Germany
	3	Spirov	USSR
	3	Talaj	Poland
Middleweight	1	Coche	France
	2	Adamczyk	Poland
	3	Oulttch	East Germany
	3	Reiter	Poland
Light-heavyweight	1	Khouboulouri	USSR
	2	Van de Walle	Belgium
	3	Schnabel	West Germany
	3	Jouvela	Yugoslavia
Heavyweight	1	Novikov	USSR
	2	Onashvilli	USSR
	3	Petrovski	Hungary
	3	Lutchitch	Yugoslavia
Open	1	Kasatchenkov	USSR
	2	Novak	Czechoslovakia
	3	Nijaradze	USSR
	3	Kokatchevitch	Yugoslavia

1977 Ludwigshafen, West Germany

Category		Name	Country
−60k	1	Pogorelov	USSR
	2	Lebaupin	France
	3	Arndt	East Germany
	3	Szabo	Romania
−65k	1	Delvingt	France
	2	Szabo	Hungary
	3	Reissmann	East Germany
	3	Biedron	Sweden
−71k	1	Nevzorov	USSR
	2	Talaj	Poland
	3	Kruger	East Germany
	3	Adams	Great Britain
−78k	1	Adamczyk	Poland
	2	Heinke	East Germany
	3	Tchoullyan	France
	3	Merhenke	West Germany
−86k	1	Volossov	USSR
	2	Rothlisberger	Switzerland
	3	Bielawski	Poland
	3	Ultsch	East Germany
−95k	1	Lorenz	East Germany
	2	Van de Walle	Belgium
	3	Schnabel	West Germany
	3	Radburn	Great Britain
+95k	1	Rouge	France
	2	Nijaradze	USSR
	3	Adelaar	Holland
	3	Zuckschwerdt	East Germany
Open	1	Parisi	France
	2	Zuckschwerdt	East Germany
	3	Tchotchichvili	USSR
	3	Van de Walle	Belgium

1978 Helsinki, Finland

Category		Name	Country
−60k	1	Mariani	Italy
	2	Szabo	Romania
	3	Arndt	East Germany
	3	Pogorelov	USSR
−65k	1	Reissmann	East Germany
	2	Solodouchin	USSR
	3	Kosic	Yugoslavia
	3	Tuncsik	Hungary
−71k	1	Krueger	East Germany
	2	Doerbandt	West Germany
	3	Adams	Great Britain
	3	Molnar	Hungary
−78k	1	Heinke	East Germany
	2	Adamczyk	Poland
	3	Jatowtt	Austria
	3	Tchoullyan	France
−86k	1	Jatskevitch	USSR
	2	Ultsch	East Germany
	3	Roethlisberger	Switzerland
	3	Frank	West Germany
−95k	1	Lorenz	East Germany
	2	Parisi	France
	3	Van de Walle	Belgium
	3	Gourine	USSR
+95k	1	Adelaar	Holland
	2	Varga	Hungary
	3	Rouge	France
	3	Novikov	USSR
Open	1	Lorenz	East Germany
	2	Rouge	France
	3	Varga	Hungary
	3	Nizharadze	USSR

1979 Brussels, Belgium

Category		Name	Country
−60k	1	Mariani	Italy
	2	Grobelin	West Germany
	3	Reiter	Austria
	3	Jemisz	USSR
−65k	1	Solodouchin	USSR
	2	Rohleder	West Germany
	3	Vlad	Romania
	3	Delvingt	France
−71k	1	Adams	Great Britain
	2	Gamba	Italy
	3	Babanow	USSR
	3	Krueger	East Germany
−78k	1	Heinke	East Germany
	2	Khabarelli	USSR
	3	Adamczyk	Poland
	3	Toma	Romania
−86k	1	Roethlisberger	Switzerland
	2	Obadov	Yugoslavia
	3	Kiss	Hungary
	3	Ultsch	East Germany
−95k	1	Khouboulouri	USSR
	2	Van de Walle	Belgium
	3	Neureuther	East Germany
	3	Koestenberger	Austria
+95k	1	Rouge	France
	2	Kuzniecow	USSR
	3	Adelaar	Holland
	3	Varge	Hungary
Open	1	Tiurin	USSR
	2	Parisi	France
	3	Radburn	Great Britain
	3	Van de Walle	Belgium

1980 Vienna, Austria

Category		Name	Country
−60k	1	Mariani	Italy
	2	Reiter	Austria
	3	Arndt	East Germany
	3	Rey	France
−65k	1	Reissmann	East Germany
	2	Tarakonov	USSR
	3	Nicolae	Romania
	3	Gelencser	Hungary
−71k	1	Vlad	Romania
	2	Bowles	Great Britain
	3	Lehmann	East Germany
	3	Babanov	USSR
−78k	1	Adams	Great Britain
	2	Heinke	East Germany
	3	Tchoullyan	France
	3	Fratica	Romania
−86k	1	Yatsekevitch	USSR
	2	Seisenbacher	Austria
	3	Donelly	Great Britain
	3	Ultsch	East Germany
−95k	1	Rouge	France
	2	Lorenz	East Germany
	3	Van de Walle	Belgium
	3	Kharchiladze	USSR
+95k	1	Tourine	USSR
	2	Varga	Hungary
	3	Adelaar	Holland
	3	Parisi	France
Open	1	Van de Walle	Belgium
	2	Parisi	France
	3	Novikov	USSR
	3	Kocman	Czechoslovakia

1981 Debrecen, Hungary

Category		Name	Country
−60k	1	Dziemianiuk	Poland
	2	Szabo	Romania
	3	Petrikov	Czechoslovakia
	3	Maurel	France
−65k	1	Likolae	Romania
	2	Rey	France
	3	Gardell	Spain
	3	Reiter	Austria
−71k	1	Lehmann	East Germany
	2	Nagysolymosi	Hungary
	3	Toplicean	Romania
	3	Nedkov	Bulgaria
−78k	1	Petrov	Bulgaria
	2	Novotny	Czechoslovakia
	3	Khabarelli	USSR
	3	Sadej	Poland
−86k	1	Bodaveli	USSR
	2	Tchoullyan	France
	3	Frank	West Germany
	3	Gyani	Hungary
−95k	1	Vachon	France
	2	Khouboulouri	USSR
	3	Van de Walle	Belgium
	3	Rettig	East Germany
+95k	1	Veritshev	USSR
	2	Zaprianov	Bulgaria
	3	Van der Groeben	West Germany
	3	Del Colombo	France
Open	1	Reszko	Poland
	2	Wilhelm	Holland
	3	Ozsvar	Hungary
	3	Schnabel	West Germany

1982 Rostock, USSR

Category		Name	Country
−60k	1	Tletseri	USSR
	2	Ghertchev	Bulgaria
	3	Stollberg	East Germany
	3	Dziemianiuk	Poland
−65k	1	Reissmann	East Germany
	2	Rey	France
	3	Reiter	Austria
	3	Pawlowski	Poland
−71k	1	Gamba	Italy
	2	Lehmann	East Germany
	3	Tuma	Czechoslovakia
	3	Parchiev	USSR
−78k	1	Fratica	Romania
	2	Khabarelli	USSR
	3	Adams	Great Britain
	3	Sadej	Poland
−86k	1	Jachkevich	USSR
	2	Vecchi	Italy
	3	Ultsch	East Germany
	3	Gyanyi	Hungary
−95k	1	Kostenberger	Austria
	2	Neureuther	West Germany
	3	Molnar	Hungary
	3	Vachon	France
+95k	1	Stohr	East Germany
	2	Parisi	France
	3	Veritchev	USSR
	3	Ozsvar	Hungary
Open	1	Turin	USSR
	2	Ozsvar	Hungary
	3	Schnabel	West Germany
	3	Olhorn	East Germany

1983 Paris, France

Category		Name	Country
−60k	1	Tletseri	USSR
	2	Dziemianiuk	Poland
	3	Jupke	West Germany
	3	Stollberg	East Germany
−65k	1	Rey	France
	2	Kris	Czechoslovakia
	3	Soloduchin	USSR
	3	Pawlowski	Poland
−71k	1	Melillo	France
	2	Gamba	Italy
	3	Lehmann	East Germany
	3	Stranz	West Germany
−78k	1	Adams	Great Britain
	2	Myllyla	Finland
	3	Khabarelli	USSR
	3	Sadej	Poland
−86k	1	Pesniak	USSR
	2	Seisenbacher	Austria
	3	Ultsch	West Germany
	3	Vecchi	Italy
−95k	1	Divisenko	USSR
	2	Vachon	France
	3	Van de Walle	Belgium
	3	Neureuther	West Germany
+95k	1	Biktachev	USSR
	2	Zaprianov	Bulgaria
	3	Parisi	France
	3	Van der Groeben	West Germany
Open	1	Parisi	France
	2	Van de Walle	Belgium
	3	Salonen	Finland
	3	Veritchev	USSR

1984 Liege, Belgium

Category		Name	Country
−60k	1	Tletseri	USSR
	2	Mariani	Italy
	3	Sotillo	Spain
	3	Roux	France
−65k	1	Alexandre	France
	2	Kriz	Czechoslovakia
	3	Chanson	Switzerlan
	3	Gawthorpe	Great Britain
−71k	1	Namgalauri	USSR
	2	Dyot	France
	3	Nagi	Romania
	3	Lorente	Spain
−78k	1	Adams	Great Britain
	2	Fogarasi	Hungary
	3	Novak	France
	3	Merulov	USSR
−86k	1	Pesnyak	USSR
	2	Borawski	East Germany
	3	Seisenbacher	Austria
	3	Spijkers	Holland
−95k	1	Neureuther	West Germany
	2	Van de Walle	Belgium
	3	Kostenberger	Austria
	3	Vachon	France
+95k	1	Van der Groeben	West Germany
	2	Pufal	East Germany
	3	Wilhelm	Holland
	3	Kocman	Czechoslovakia
Open	1	Parisi	France
	2	Verichev	USSR
	3	Cioc	Romania
	3	Van de Walle	Belgium

1985 Hamar, Norway

Category		Name	Country
−60k	1	Tletseri	USSR
	2	Dahi	Romania
	3	Roux	France
	3	Sotillo	Spain
−65k	1	Serban	Romania
	2	Alexander	France
	3	Haggqvist	Sweden
	3	Palkschek	East Germany
−71k	1	Namgalauri	USSR
	2	Hajtos	Hungary
	3	Brown	Great Britain
	3	Melillo	France
−78k	1	Adams	Great Britain
	2	Legien	Poland
	3	Kjellin	Sweden
	3	Nowak	France
−86k	1	Pesniak	USSR
	2	Bazynski	West Germany
	3	Petrov	Bulgaria
	3	Seisenbacher	Austria
−95k	1	Van de Walle	Belgium
	2	Vachon	France
	3	Neureuther	West Germany
	3	Preschel	East Germany
+95k	1	Veritchev	USSR
	2	Van der Groeben	West Germany
	3	Salonen	Finland
	3	Kusmuk	Yugoslavia
Open	1	Van der Groeben	West Germany
	2	Biktachev	USSR
	3	Gordon	Great Britain
	3	Basik	Poland

1986 Belgrade, Yugoslavia

Category		Name	Country
−60k	1	Csak	Hungary
	2	Jupke	West Germany
	3	Tletseri	USSR
	3	Roux	France
−65k	1	Sokolov	USSR
	2	Brenner	West Germany
	3	Pawlovski	Poland
	3	Alexandre	France
−71k	1	Haitosz	Hungary
	2	Brown	Great Britain
	3	Gamba	Italy
	3	Blach	Poland
−78k	1	Wieneke	West Germany
	2	Pietri	France
	3	Pink	East Germany
	3	Legien	Poland
−86k	1	Seisenbacher	Austria
	2	Spykers	Holland
	3	Canu	France
	3	Gyani	Hungary
−95k	1	Van de Walle	Belgium
	2	Vachon	France
	3	Sosna	Czechoslovakia
	3	Kolanovski	Poland
+95k	1	Wilhelm	Holland
	2	Stohr	East Germany
	3	Verichev	USSR
	3	Jehle	Switzerland
Open	1	Stohr	East Germany
	2	Seisenbacher	Austria
	3	Vachon	France
	3	Veritsev	USSR

1987, Paris, France

Category		Name	Country
−60k	1	Roux	France
	2	Tletseri	USSR
	3	Eckersley	Great Britain
	3	Dietz	West Germany
−65k	1	Hansen	France
	2	Becanovic	Yugoslavia
	3	Kosmylin	USSR
	3	Bujko	Hungary
−71k	1	Blach	Poland
	2	Melillo	France
	3	Stranz	West Germany
	3	Loll	East Germany
−78k	1	Varaev	USSR
	2	Berthet	France
	3	Reiter	Austria
	3	Sadej	Poland
−86k	1	Canu	France
	2	White	Great Britain
	3	Poddubny	USSR
	3	Seisenbacher	Austria
−95k	1	Kurtanidze	USSR
	2	Vachon	France
	3	Van de Walle	Belgium
	3	Meiling	West Germany
+95k	1	Cioc	Romania
	2	Jehle	Switzerland
	3	Van der Groeben	West Germany
	3	Kibordzalidze	USSR
Open	1	Veritchev	USSR
	2	Vachon	France
	3	Basik	Poland
	3	Plate	West Germany

WOMEN'S EUROPEAN CHAMPIONSHIPS

1975 Munich, West Germany

Category		Name	Country
−48k	1	Hrovat	Austria
	2	Campo	Spain
	3	Lecocq	France
	3	Lof	Sweden
−52k	1	Herzog	France
	2	Vasic	Yugoslavia
	3	Matteman	Holland
	3	Winklbauer	Austria
−56	1	Happ	West Germany
	2	Luzzi	Italy
	3	Reifgraber	Austria
	3	Callu	Belgium
−61k	1	Rottier	France
	2	Mil	Belgium
	3	Vringer	Holland
	3	Nicol	Great Britain
−66k	1	Fouillet	France
	2	Triadou	France
	3	Weiss	West Germany
	3	Di Toma	Italy
−72k	1	Pierre	France
	2	Kuttner	West Germany
	3	Harmon	Great Britain
	3	Cobb	Great Britain
+72k	1	Child	Great Britain
	2	De Cal	Italy
	3	McKenna	Great Britain
	3	Kieburg	West Germany
Open	1	Pierre	France
	2	Fouillet	France
	3	Di Toma	Italy
	3	Kieburg	West Germany

1976 Vienna, Austria

Category		Name	Country
−48k	1	Bridge	Great Britain
	2	Davico	Italy
	3	Hillesheim	West Germany
	3	Tripet	France
−52k	1	Hrovat	Austria
	2	Winklbauer	Austria
	3	Matteman	Holland
	3	Dayez	France
−56k	1	Happ	West Germany
	2	Moyano	Spain
	3	Luzzi	Italy
	3	Trucios	France
−61k	1	Rottier	France
	2	Angelovic	Yugoslavia
	3	Mil	Belgium
	3	Hilger	West Germany
−66k	1	Fouillet	France
	2	Triadou	France
	3	Di Toma	Italy
	3	Czerwinsky	West Germany
−72k	1	Pierre	France
	2	Jirkal	Austria
	3	Salzmann	Switzerland
	3	Jodogne	Belgium
+72k	1	Kieburg	West Germany
	2	Cobb	Great Britain
	3	Parenti	Italy
	3	De Cal	Italy
Open	1	Di Toma	Italy
	2	Thomas	Holland
	3	Pierre	France
	3	Kieburg	West Germany

1977 Arlon, Belgium

Category		Name	Country
−48k	1	Hillesheim	West Germany
	2	Mazaud	France
	3	Bouthemy	France
	3	Homminga	Holland
−52k	1	Hrovat	Austria
	2	Luzzi	Italy
	3	Peeters	Belgium
	3	Fontana	Italy
−56k	1	Happ	West Germany
	2	Ljundberg	Sweden
	3	Van der Meulen	Holland
	4	Meulemans	Belgium
−61k	1	Berg	West Germany
	2	Thomas	Holland
	3	Hilger	West Germany
	3	Rottier	France
−66k	1	Czerwinsky	West Germany
	2	Mil	Belgium
	3	Suc	France
	3	Droegekamp	West Germany
−72k	1	Pierre	France
	2	Costa	Spain
	3	Gerber	West Germany
	3	Classen	West Germany
+72k	1	Kieburg	West Germany
	2	Schmutzer	Austria
	3	Samery	France
	3	Olsson	Sweden
Open	1	Triadou	France
	2	Schroth	Austria
	3	Pierre	France
	3	Kieburg	West Germany

1978 Cologne, West Germany

Category		Name	Country
−48k	1	Bridge	Great Britain
	2	Vial	France
	3	Jankowski	West Germany
	3	Iglesias	Spain
−52k	1	Hrovat	Austria
	2	Moyano-Luque	Spain
	3	Herzog	France
	3	Nguyen	Switzerland
−56k	1	Winklbauer	Austria
	2	Netherwood	Great Britain
	3	Ricciato	Italy
	3	Ljungberg	Sweden
−61k	1	Berg	West Germany
	2	Rottier	France
	3	Peeters	Belgium
	3	Monti	Italy
−66k	1	Grueger	West Germany
	2	Rothacher	Switzerland
	3	Fouillet	France
	3	Mil	Belgium
−72k	1	Classen	West Germany
	2	Pierre	France
	3	Venmeer	Holland
	4	Malley	Great Britain
+72k	1	Kieburg	West Germany
	2	Schmutzer	Austria
	3	Parenti	Italy
	3	Samery	France
Open	1	Rothacher	Switzerland
	2	Triadou	France
	3	Mil	Belgium
	3	Malley	Great Britain

1979 Kerkrade, Holland

Category		Name	Country
−48k	1	Bouthemy	France
	2	Homminga	Holland
	3	Grimm	West Germany
	3	Napolitano	Italy
−52k	1	Hrovat	Austria
	2	Matteman	Holland
	3	Movano-Luque	Spain
	3	McCarthy	Great Britain
−56k	1	Winklbauer	Austria
	2	Ricciato	Italy
	3	Ljungberg	Sweden
	3	Trucios	France
−61k	1	Deydier	France
	2	Netherwood	Great Britain
	3	Di Toma	Italy
	3	Berg	West Germany
−66k	1	Mil	Belgium
	2	Bennet	Great Britain
	3	Iglesias	France
	3	Krueger	West Germany
−72k	1	Triadou	France
	2	Salzmann	Switzerland
	3	Classen	West Germany
	3	Litscher	Austria
+72k	1	Kieburg	West Germany
	2	De Cal	Italy
	3	Samery	France
	3	Schmutzer	Austria
Open	1	Classen	West Germany
	2	Pierre	France
	3	Malley	Great Britain
	3	Parenti	Italy

1980 Udine, Italy

Category		Name	Country
−48k	1	Bridge	Great Britain
	2	Napolitano	Italy
	3	Bechepay	France
	3	Hillesheim	West Germany
−52k	1	Montaguti	Italy
	2	McCarthy	Great Britain
	3	Hrovat	Austria
	3	Smilianic	Yugoslavia
−56k	1	Winklbauer	Austria
	2	Beeks	Holland
	3	Nguyen	Switzerland
	3	Doyle	Great Britain
−61k	1	Di Toma	Italy
	2	Deydier	France
	3	Angelovic	Yugoslavia
	3	Peeters	Belgium
−66k	1	Pierre	France
	2	Amerighi	Italy
	3	Mil	Belgium
	3	Mallens	Holland
−72k	1	Triadou	France
	2	Berghmans	Belgium
	3	Classen	West Germany
	3	Malley	Great Britain
+72k	1	De Cal	Italy
	2	Fouillet	France
	3	Kieburg	West Germany
	3	Ford	Great Britain
Open	1	Classen	West Germany
	2	Berghmans	Belgium
	3	Malley	Great Britain
	3	Fouillet	France

1981 Madrid, Spain

Category		Name	Country
−48k	1	Friedrich	West Germany
	2	De Novellis	Italy
	3	Briggs	Great Britain
	3	Nadj	Yugoslavia
−52k	1	Hrovat	Austria
	2	Doyle	Great Britain
	3	Moyano	Spain
	3	Van Weyen	Holland
−56k	1	Winklbauer	Austria
	2	Solbach	West Germany
	3	Beeks	Holland
	3	Zimbaro	Italy
−61k	1	Hughes	Great Britain
	2	Di Toma	Italy
	3	Berg	West Germany
	3	Rottier	France
−66k	1	Mil	Belgium
	2	Schreiber	West Germany
	3	Andersson	Sweden
	3	Simon	Austria
−72k	1	Triadou	France
	2	Classen	West Germany
	3	Berghmans	Belgium
	3	Posch	Austria
+72k	1	De Cal	Italy
	2	Kieburg	West Germany
	3	Vigneron	France
	3	Van Unen	Holland
Open	1	Classen	West Germany
	2	Berghmans	Belgium
	3	Van Unen	Holland
	3	Motta	Italy

1982 Oslo, Norway

Category		Name	Country
−48k	1	Briggs	Great Britain
	2	De Novellis	Italy
	3	Colignon	France
	3	Ronkainen	Finland
−52k	1	Hrovat	Austria
	2	Doyle	Great Britain
	3	Lof	Sweden
	3	Doger	France
−56k	1	Rodriguez	France
	2	Limerick	Sweden
	3	Krasser	Switzerland
	3	Winklbauer	Austria
−61k	1	Reiter	Austria
	2	Han	Holland
	3	Ritschel	West Germany
	3	Rottier	France
−66k	1	Simon	Austria
	2	Netherwood	Great Britain
	3	Kruger	West Germany
	3	Dekarz	France
−72k	1	Triadou	France
	2	Classen	West Germany
	3	Berg	Sweden
	3	Ines	Spain
+72k	1	Unen	Holland
	2	Kieburg	West Germany
	3	Vigneron	France
	3	De Cal	Italy
Open	1	Simon	Austria
	2	Meggelen	Holland
	3	Cortavitarte	Spain
	3	Classen	West Germany

1983 Genoa, Italy

Category		Name	Country
−48k	1	Briggs	Great Britain
	2	Valvano	Italy
	3	Friedrich	West Germany
	3	Boffin	France
−52k	1	Doyle	Great Britain
	2	Doger	France
	3	Hrovat	Austria
	3	Montaguti	Italy
−56k	1	Winklbauer	Austria
	2	Philips	West Germany
	3	Beeks	Holland
	3	Rodriguez	France
−61k	1	Hughes	Great Britain
	2	Ritschel	West Germany
	3	Rottier	France
	3	Reiter	Austria
−66k	1	Di Toma	Italy
	2	Netherwood	Great Britain
	3	Kranzl	Austria
	3	Schreiber	West Germany
−72k	1	Berghmans	Belgium
	2	Vigneron	France
	3	Classen	West Germany
	3	Posch	Austria
+72k	1	Motta	Italy
	2	Lupino	France
	3	Van Unen	Holland
	3	Wantling	Great Britain
Open	1	Berghmans	Belgium
	2	Motta	Italy
	3	Classen	West Germany
	3	Posch	Austria

1984 Pirmasens, West Germany

Category		Name	Country
−48k	1	Briggs	Great Britain
	2	Boffin	France
	3	Friedrich	West Germany
	3	Veguillas	Spain
−52k	1	Hrovat	Austria
	2	Montaguti	Italy
	3	Moyano	Spain
	3	Heuvelmans	Holland
−56k	1	Bell	Great Britain
	2	Winklbauer	Austria
	3	Rodriguez	France
	3	Phillips	West Germany
−61k	1	Rottier	France
	2	Wahnsiedler	West Germany
	3	Di Toma	Italy
	3	Hughes	Great Britain
−66k	1	Deydier	France
	2	Hartl	Austria
	3	Lieckens	Belgium
	3	De Kok	Holland
−72k	1	Classen	West Germany
	2	Cicot	France
	3	Hayden	Great Britain
	3	Antoine	Belgium
+72k	1	Van Unen	Holland
	2	Lupino	France
	3	Arsenovic	Yugoslavia
	3	Motta	Italy
Open	1	Lupino	France
	2	Motta	Italy
	3	Bradshaw	Great Britain
	3	Kutz	France

1985 Landskrona, Sweden

Category		Name	Country
−48k	1	Colignon	France
	2	Friedrich	West Germany
	3	Briody	Great Britain
	3	Chodakowska	Poland
−52k	1	Doger	France
	2	Kantojarvi	Sweden
	3	Briggs	Great Britain
	3	Hrovat	Austria
−56k	1	Rodriguez	France
	2	Winklbauer	Austria
	3	Bell	Great Britain
	3	Gontowicz	Poland
−61k	1	Olechnowicz	Poland
	2	Ritschel	West Germany
	3	De Brabander	Belgium
	3	Hughes	Great Britain
−66k	1	Deydier	France
	2	Hartl	Austria
	3	Karlsson	Sweden
	3	Bellon	Spain
−72k	1	Berghmans	Belgium
	2	Classen	West Germany
	3	Posch	Austria
	3	Lupino	France
+72k	1	Bradshaw	Great Britain
	2	Vainio	Finland
	3	Van Unen	Holland
	3	Motta	Italy
Open	1	Van Unen	Holland
	2	Posch	Austria
	3	Hayden	Great Britain
	3	Maksymow	Poland

1986 Crystal Palace, Great Britain

Category		Name	Country
−48k	1	Briggs	Great Britain
	2	Veguillas	Spain
	3	Vand De Pas	Holland
	3	Biffin	France
−52k	1	Brun	France
	2	Hrovat	Austria
	3	Doyle	Great Britain
	3	Majdan	Poland
−56k	1	Rodriguez	France
	2	Soraci	Italy
	3	Gontowicz	Poland
	3	Hughes	Great Britain
−61k	1	Bell	Great Britain
	2	De Brabander	Belgium
	3	Geraud	France
	3	Ritschel	West Germany
−66k	1	Deydier	France
	2	Schreiber	West Germany
	3	Fiorentini	Italy
	3	Karlsson	Sweden
−72k	1	De Kok	Holland
	2	Classen	West Germany
	3	Meignan	France
	3	Berghmans	Belgium
+72k	1	Maksymow	Poland
	2	Bradshaw	Great Britain
	3	Paques	France
	3	Sigmund	West Germany
Open	1	De Kok	Holland
	2	Hartl	Austria
	3	Kutz	West Germany
	3	Cicot	France

1987 Paris, France

Category		Name	Country
−48k	1	Briggs	Great Britain
	2	Chodakowska	Poland
	3	Van den Pas	Holland
	3	Dupont	France
−52k	1	Brun	France
	2	Hrovat	Austria
	3	Giunji	Italy
	3	Rendle	Great Britain
−56k	1	Arnaud	France
	2	Hughes	Great Britain
	3	Philips	West Germany
	3	Gontowicz	Poland
−61k	1	Olechnowicz	Poland
	2	Gross	Holland
	3	Ritschel	West Germany
	3	Bell	Great Britain
−66k	1	Han	Holland
	2	Keuger	West Germany
	3	Adamczyk	Poland
	3	Lionnet	France
−72k	1	De Kok	Holland
	2	Berghmans	Belgium
	3	Drzewiecka	Poland
	3	Colagrossi	Italy
+72k	1	Paque	France
	2	Seriese	Holland
	3	Medina	Spain
	3	Kutz	West Germany
Open	1	Berghmans	Belgium
	2	Sigmund	West Germany
	3	De Kok	Holland
	3	Meignan	France

MEN'S WORLD CHAMPIONSHIPS

1956 Tokyo, Japan

Category		Name	Country
Open	1	Natsui	Japan
	2	Yoshimatsu	Japan
	3	Geesink	Holland
	3	Courtine	France

1958 Tokyo, Japan

Category		Name	Country
Open	1	Sone	Japan
	2	Kaminaga	Japan
	3	Yamashiki	Japan
	3	Pariset	France

1961 Paris, France

Category		Name	Country
Open	1	Geesink	Holland
	2	Sone	Japan
	3	Koga	Japan
	3	Pae	S. Korea

1964 Tokyo, Japan

Category		Name	Country
Open	1	Geesink	Holland
	2	Kaminaga	Japan
	3	Glahn	West Germany
	3	Boronovski	Australia

1965 Rio de Janeiro, Brazil

Category		Name	Country
Lightweight	1	Matsuda	Japan
	2	Minatoya	Japan
	3	Kid Soon Park	S. Korea
	3	Stepanov	USSR
Middleweight	1	Okano	Japan
	2	Yamanaka	Japan
	3	Tai	S. Korea
	3	Bregman	USA
Heavyweight	1	Geesink	Holland
	2	Matsunaga	Japan
	3	Sakaguchi	Japan
	3	Rogers	Canada
Open	1	Inokuma	Japan
	2	Kibrosachvili	USSR
	3	Snyders	Holland
	3	Kiknadze	USSR

1967 Salt Lake City, USA

Category		Name	Country
Lightweight	1	Shigeoka	Japan
	2	Matsuda	Japan
	3	Susline	USSR
	3	Kim	S. Korea
Light-middleweight	1	Minatoya	Japan
	2	Kid Soon Park	S. Korea
	3	Nakatani	Japan
	3	Chung Sam Park	S. Korea
Middleweight	1	Maruki	Japan
	2	Poglajen	Holland
	3	Enshu	Japan
	3	Jacks	Great Britain
Light-heavyweight	1	Nobuyuki Sato	Japan
	2	Osamu Sato	Japan
	3	Eugster	Holland
	3	Herrmann	West Germany
Heavyweight	1	Ruska	Holland
	2	Maejima	Japan
	3	Matsuzaka	Japan
	3	Kiknadze	USSR
Open	1	Matsunaga	Japan
	2	Glahn	West Germany
	3	Herrmann	West Germany
	3	Shinomaki	Japan

1969 Mexico City, Mexico

Category		Name	Country
Lightweight	1	Sonoda	Japan
	2	Nomura	Japan
	3	Susline	USSR
	3	Chul	S. Korea
Light-middleweight	1	Minatoya	Japan
	2	Kono	Japan
	3	Rudmann	USSR
	3	Bok	S. Korea
Middleweight	1	Sonoda	Japan
	2	Hirao	Japan
	3	Poklajen	Holland
	3	Ip	S. Korea
Light-heavyweight	1	Sasahara	Japan
	2	Herrmann	West Germany
	3	Kawabata	Japan
	3	Pokataev	USSR
Heavyweight	1	Suma	Japan
	2	Glahn	West Germany
	3	Matsunaga	Japan
	3	Onashvilli	USSR
Open	1	Shinomaki	Japan
	2	Ruska	Holland
	3	Sato	Japan
	3	Eugster	Holland

1971 Ludwigshafen, West Germany

Category		Name	Country
Lightweight	1	Kawaguchi	Japan
	2	Nomura	Japan
	3	Susline	USSR
	3	Sam	S. Korea
Light-middleweight	1	Tsuzawa	Japan
	2	Minatoya	Japan
	3	Hoetger	East Germany
	3	Zajkowski	Poland
Middleweight	1	Fujii	Japan
	2	Shigematsu	Japan
	3	Auffray	France
	3	Starbrook	Great Britain
Light-heavyweight	1	Sasahara	Japan
	2	Sato	Japan
	3	Ishii	Brazil
	3	Howiller	East Germany
Heavyweight	1	Ruska	Holland
	2	Glahn	West Germany
	3	Iwata	Japan
	3	Remfry	Great Britain
Open	1	Shinomaki	Japan
	2	Kuznetsov	USSR
	3	Sekine	Japan
	3	Glahn	West Germany

1973 Lausanne, Switzerland

Category		Name	Country
Lightweight	1	Minami	Japan
	2	Kawaguchi	Japan
	3	Rodriguez	Cuba
	3	Pitchelauri	USSR
Light-middleweight	1	Nomura	Japan
	2	Hoetger	East Germany
	3	Novikov	USSR
	3	Yoshimura	Japan
Middleweight	1	Fujii	Japan
	2	Sonoda	Japan
	3	Reiter	Poland
	3	Look	East Germany
Light-heavyweight	1	Sato	Japan
	2	Uegushi	Japan
	3	Starbrook	Great Britain
	3	Lorenz	East Germany
Heavyweight	1	Takagi	Japan
	2	Nichiradze	USSR
	3	Novikov	USSR
	3	Remfry	Great Britain
Open	1	Ninomiya	Japan
	2	Uemura	Japan
	3	Glahn	West Germany
	3	Zuckschwerdt	East Germany

1975 Vienna, Austria

Category		Name	Country
Lightweight	1	Minami	Japan
	2	Kashiwasaki	Japan
	3	Reissmann	East Germany
	3	Mariani	Italy
Light-middleweight	1	Nevzorov	USSR
	2	Dvoinikov	USSR
	3	Kuramoto	Japan
	3	Akimoto	Japan
Middleweight	1	Fujii	Japan
	2	Hara	Japan
	3	Adamczyk	Poland
	3	Coche	France
Light-heavyweight	1	Rouge	France
	2	Ishibashi	Japan
	3	Karschiladze	USSR
	3	Betanov	USSR
Heavyweight	1	Endo	Japan
	2	Novikov	USSR
	3	Takagi	Japan
	3	Pak	S. Korea
Open	1	Uemura	Japan
	2	Ninomiya	Japan
	3	Chochoshvili	USSR
	3	Lorenz	East Germany

1979 Paris, France

Category		Name	Country
Bantamweight	1	Rey	France
	2	Jong	S. Korea
	3	Mariani	Italy
	3	Moriwaki	Japan
Featherweight	1	Solodouchin	USSR
	2	Delvingt	France
	3	Pawlowski	Poland
	3	Sahara	Japan
Lightweight	1	Katsuki	Japan
	2	Gamba	Italy
	3	Namgalauri	USSR
	3	Adams	Great Britian
Light-middleweight	1	Fujii	Japan
	2	Tchoullyan	France
	3	Heinke	East Germany
	3	Park	S. Korea
Middleweight	1	Ultsch	East Germany
	2	Sanchis	France
	3	Takahashi	Japan
	3	Carmona	Brazil
Light-heavyweight	1	Khouboulouri	USSR
	2	Van de Walle	Belgium
	3	Numan	Holland
	3	Neureuther	West Germany
Heavyweight	1	Yamashita	Japan
	2	Rouge	France
	3	Varga	Hungary
	3	Ki	S. Korea
Open	1	Endo	Japan
	2	Kuznetsov	USSR
	3	Rouge	France
	3	Kovacevic	Yugoslavia

1981 Maastricht, Holland

Category		Name	Country
Bantamweight	1	Moriwaki	Japan
	2	Petrikov	Czechoslovakia
	3	Mariani	Italy
	3	Takahashi	Canada
Featherweight	1	Kashiwasaki	Japan
	2	Nicolae	Romania
	3	Ponomarev	USSR
	3	Hwang	S. Korea
Lightweight	1	Ha	S. Korea
	2	Dyot	France
	3	Vujevic	Yugoslavia
	3	Lehmann	East Germany
Light-middleweight	1	Adams	Great Britain
	2	Kase	Japan
	3	Petrov	Bulgaria
	3	Doherty	Canada
Middleweight	1	Tchoullyan	France
	2	Nose	Japan
	3	Ultsch	East Germany
	3	Bodaveli	USSR
Light-heavyweight	1	Khouboulouri	USSR
	2	Van de Walle	Belgium
	3	Vachon	France
	3	Ha	S. Korea
Heavyweight	1	Yamashita	Japan
	2	Veritchev	USSR
	3	Kocman	Czechoslovakia
	3	Salonen	Finland
Open	1	Yamashita	Japan
	2	Reszko	Poland
	3	Van de Walle	Belgium
	3	Ozsvar	Hungary

1983 Moscow, USSR

Category		Name	Country
Bantamweight	1	Tletseri	USSR
	2	Bujko	Hungary
	3	Haraguchi	Japan
	3	Stollberg	East Germany
Featherweight	1	Soloduchin	USSR
	2	Matsuoka	Japan
	3	Pavlovski	Poland
	3	Rozati	Italy
Lightweight	1	Nakanishi	Japan
	2	Gamba	Italy
	3	Namgalauri	USSR
	3	Stranz	West Germany
Light-middleweight	1	Hikage	Japan
	2	Adams	Great Britain
	3	Khabarelli	USSR
	3	Fratica	Romania
Middleweight	1	Ultsch	East Germany
	2	Canu	France
	3	Berland	USA
	3	Nose	Japan
Light-heavyweight	1	Preschel	East Germany
	2	Divisenko	USSR
	3	Neureuther	West Germany
	3	Van de Walle	Belgium
Heavyweight	1	Yamashita	Japan
	2	Vilhem	Holland
	3	Stohr	East Germany
	3	Cioc	Romania
Open	1	Saito	Japan
	2	Kocman	Czechoslovakia
	3	Ozsvar	Hungary
	3	Van de Walle	Belgium

1985 Seoul, S. Korea

Category		Name	Country
−60k	1	Hosokawa	Japan
	2	Jupke	West Germany
	3	Bujko	Hungary
	3	Tletseri	USSR
−65k	1	Sokolov	USSR
	2	Lee Kyung Keun	S. Korea
	3	Gawthorpe	Great Britain
	3	Matsuoka	Japan
−71k	1	Ahn Byung Keun	S. Korea
	2	Swain	USA
	3	Stranz	West Germany
	3	Blach	Poland
−78k	1	Hikage	Japan
	2	Denhmigen	East Germany
	3	Shestakov	USSR
	3	Adams	Great Britain
−86k	1	Seisenbacher	Austria
	2	Petrov	Bulgaria
	3	Canu	France
	3	Pesniak	USSR
−95k	1	Sugai	Japan
	2	Ha	S. Korea
	3	Neureuther	West Germany
	3	Van de Walle	Belgium
+95k	1	Cho	S. Korea
	2	Hitoshi Saito	Japan
	3	Zaprianov	Bulgaria
	3	Veritchev	USSR
Open	1	Masaki	Japan
	2	Rashwan	Egypt
	3	Biktashev	USSR
	3	Wilhelm	Holland

WOMEN'S WORLD CHAMPIONSHIPS

1980 New York, United States

Category		Name	Country
−48k	1	Bridge	Great Britain
	2	De Novellis	Italy
	3	Colignon	France
	3	Lewis	United States
−52k	1	Hrovat	Austria
	2	Yamaguchi	Japan
	3	McCarthy	Great Britain
	3	Doger	France
−56	1	Winklbauer	Austria
	2	Panza	France
	3	Doyle	Great Britain
	3	Meulemans	Belgium
−61k	1	Staps	Holland
	2	De Toma	Italy
	3	Rottier	France
	3	Berg	West Germany
−66k	1	Simon	Austria
	2	Netherwood	Great Britain
	3	Penick	United States
	3	Peirre	France
−72k	1	Triadou	France
	2	Classen	West Germany
	3	Van Meggelen	Holland
	3	Malley	Great Britain
+72k	1	De Cal	Italy
	2	Fouillet	France
	3	Keiburg	West Germany
	3	Berghmans	Belgium
Open	1	Berghmans	Belgium
	2	Fouillet	France
	3	Classen	West Germany
	3	Fest	United States

1982 Paris, France

Category		Name	Country
−48k	1	Briggs	Great Britain
	2	Colignon	France
	3	Nakahara	Japan
	3	Bink	Holland
−52k	1	Doyle	Great Britain
	2	Yamaguchi	Japan
	3	Doger	France
	3	Boyd	Australia
−56k	1	Rodriguez	France
	2	Williams	Australia
	3	Aronoff	USA
	3	Bell	Great Britain
−61k	1	Rottier	France
	2	Solheim	Norway
	3	Peeters	Belgium
	3	Ritchel	West Germany
−66k	1	Deydier	France
	2	Kruger	West Germany
	3	Andersen	Norway
	3	Staps	Holland
−72k	1	Classen	West Germany
	2	Berghmans	Belgium
	3	Triadou	France
	3	Posch	Austria
+72k	1	Lupino	France
	2	Castro	United States
	3	Van Unen	Holland
	3	Motta	Italy
Open	1	Berghmans	Belgium
	2	Tateishi	Japan
	3	Triadou	France
	3	Sigmund	West Germany

1984 Vienna, Austria

Category		Name	Country
−48k	1	Briggs	Great Britain
	2	Colignon	France
	3	Reardon	Australia
	3	Anaya	United States
−52k	1	Yamaguchi	Japan
	2	Hrovat	Austria
	3	Boyd	Australia
	3	Majdan	Poland
−56k	1	Burns	United States
	2	Williams	Australia
	3	Winklbauer	Austria
	4	Arnaud	France
−61k	1	Hernandez	Venezuela
	2	Han	Holland
	3	Rottier	France
	3	Hashinohe	Japan
−66k	1	Deydier	France
	2	De Kok	Holland
	3	Netherwood	Great Britain
	3	Kandori	Japan
−72k	1	Berghmans	Belgium
	2	Classen	West Germany
	3	Staps	Holland
	3	Vigneron	France
+72k	1	Motta	Italy
	2	Gao	China
	3	Castro	United States
	3	Van Unen	Holland
Open	1	Berghmans	Belgium
	2	Van Unen	Holland
	3	Lupino	France
	3	Gao	China

1986 Maastricht, Holland

Category		Name	Country
−48k	1	Briggs	Great Britain
	2	Ezaki	Japan
	3	Boffin	France
	3	Zhangyun	China
−52k	1	Brun	France
	2	Yamaguchi	Japan
	3	Sook Ok	South Korea
	3	Rendle	Great Britain
−56k	1	Hughes	Great Britain
	2	Gontoqicz	Poland
	3	Rodriguez	France
	3	Gross	Holland
−61k	1	Bell	Great Britain
	2	Geraud	France
	3	Guy	New Zealand
	3	Fujimoto	Japan
−66k	1	Deydier	France
	2	Karlsson	Sweden
	3	Staps	Holland
	3	Schreiber	West Germany
−72k	1	De Kok	Holland
	2	Berghmans	Belgium
	3	Lin	China
	4	Classens	West Germany
+72k	1	Gao	China
	2	Van Unen	Holland
	3	Santini	Puerto Rico
	3	Paque	France
Open	1	Berghmans	Belgium
	2	Ling Li	China
	3	Meignan	France
	3	Kutz	West Germany

OLYMPIC GAMES

1964 Tokyo, Japan

Category		Name	Country
−68k	1	Nakatani	Japan
	2	Haenni	Switzerland
	3	Stepanov	USSR
	3	Bogolubov	USSR
−80k	1	Okano	Japan
	2	Hoffmann	West Germany
	3	Bregman	USA
	3	Kim	S. Korea
+80k	1	Inokuma	Japan
	2	Rogers	Canada
	3	Kiknadze	USSR
	3	Chikviladze	USSR
Open	1	Geesink	Holland
	2	Kaminaga	Japan
	3	Boronovskis	Australia
	3	Glahn	West Germany

1972 Munich, West Germany

Category		Name	Country
−63k	1	Kawaguchi	Japan
	2	—	—
	3	Mounier	France
	3	Y Kim	N. Korea
−70k	1	Nomura	Japan
	2	Zajkowski	Poland
	3	Hoetger	East Germany
	3	Novikov	USSR
−80k	1	Sekine	Japan
	2	S. Oh	Korea
	3	Jacks	Great Britain
	3	Coche	France
−93k	1	Chochoshvili	USSR
	2	Starbrook	Great Britain
	3	Ishii	Brazil
	3	Barth	West Germany
+93k	1	Ruska	Holland
	2	Glahn	West Germany
	3	Onashvili	USSR
	3	Nishimura	Japan
Open	1	Ruska	Holland
	2	Kusnezov	USSR
	3	Brondani	France
	3	Parisi	France

1976 Montreal, Canada

Category		Name	Country
−63k	1	Rodriguez	Cuba
	2	Chang	S. Korea
	3	Mariani	Italy
	3	Tuncsik	Hungary
−70k	1	Nevzorov	USSR
	2	Kuramoto	Japan
	3	Vial	France
	3	Talaj	Poland
−80k	1	Sonoda	Japan
	2	Dvoinikov	USSR
	3	Obadov	Yugoslavia
	3	Yung Chul Park	S. Korea
−93k	1	Ninomiya	Japan
	2	Harshiladze	USSR
	3	Rothlisberger	Switzerland
	3	Starbrook	Great Britain
+93k	1	Novikov	USSR
	2	Neureuther	West Germany
	3	Coage	USA
	3	Endo	Japan
Open	1	Uemura	Japan
	2	Remfry	Great Britain
	3	Chochoshvilli	USSR
	3	Cho	S. Korea

1980 Moscow, USSR

Category		Name	Country
−60k	1	Rey	France
	2	Rodriguez	Cuba
	3	Emizh	USSR
	3	Kincses	Hungary
−65k	1	Soloduchin	USSR
	2	Damden	Mongolia
	3	Nedkov	Bulgaria
	3	Pawlowski	Poland
−71k	1	Gamba	Italy
	2	Adams	Great Britain
	3	Dawaadalia	Mongolia
	3	Lehmann	East Germany
−78k	1	Khabarelli	USSR
	2	Ferrer	Cuba
	3	Heinke	East Germany
	3	Tchoullyan	France
−86k	1	Roethlisberger	Switzerland
	2	Azcuy	Cuba
	3	Iatskevich	USSR
	3	Ultsch	East Germany
−95k	1	Van de Walle	Belgium
	2	Khouboulouri	USSR
	3	Lorenz	East Germany
	3	Numan	Holland
+95k	1	Parisi	France
	2	Zaprianov	Bulgaria
	3	Kockman	CSSR
	3	Kovacevic	Yugoslavia
Open	1	Lorenz	West Germany
	2	Parisi	France
	3	Mapp	Great Britain
	3	Ozsvar	Hungary